TRANSFORMATIONAL MEDITATIONS

Pastor Bryant K. Smith

Transformational Meditations

Copyright © 2022 Bryant Keith Smith and Yendi A. Anderson

ISBN: 978-1-66782-873-2
eBook ISBN: 978-1-66782-874-9

Phrases of the Day Written by Prophet Bryant Keith Smith,
Pastor of Pillars of Fire Apostolic Center

Daily Prayers Written By Yendi A. Anderson

Interior Layout By Yendi A. Anderson

Cover Concept & Design by Yendi A. Anderson & Olympia Martin

Photography By F. Calis of M-Duce Vision

Edited by Keisha Anderson – Dickey

Printed by
BookBaby

Dedication

I would like to dedicate this book to the Holy Spirit, my father, Charles Henry Smith and Slyvana Elena Holder. They lived their last days loving God, one day at a time.

Introduction

It's all about being transformed. The only way to transform is to renew one's mind with the Word of God. This tool came about, because someone needs to remind us to study God's Word. I pray this tool is effective. I want for every reader to develop a solid relationship with God. The Phrases of the Day started approximately 14 years ago, to encourage and instill knowledge in all who read them. If they ask God for understanding of the writing, He will give them an opportunity to experience His Word, which brings understanding.

Opening Prayer

Heavenly Father, we ask in the name of Jesus, that You penetrate conditioning their hearts to receive Your gift of Jesus Christ. Heavenly Father, Your word says, Heaven and Earth will pass away, but Your will, will accomplish what it was sent to do. Let Your Word marinate in our soul and create in us a clean heart and a renewed spirit.

JANUARY 1ST

TRANSFORMATIONAL MEDITATIONS

Daily Prayer

Lord, give me wisdom, that I may know the truth.
Open my heart and my mind and my spirit that
I will know what is of You and what isn't.

"Scripture for the Day"
Romans Chapters 1-2

PHRASE OF THE DAY

Your thoughts determine your character. Be careful of
your thoughts, they may break into words at any minute.
The first person you lead is you. Master your mind.

JANUARY 2ND

TRANSFORMATIONAL MEDITATIONS

"Scripture for the Day"
Genesis Chapters 1-3

PHRASE OF THE DAY

One of the ways for the enemy to gain access is selfishness.
We will use the excuse; they are doing it so why can't
I? Pride will keep you from repenting and correction.
The longer you push away correction the deeper the
root of bitterness grows. I plead the blood of Jesus over
the blinders that you may see the enemy's plan.

Daily Prayer

Lord, let pride not get the best of me. Help me to
have a heart that is filled with humility. Let my
lips not boast or brag and let me sincerely give
praise, honor and glory to You and You alone.

TRANSFORMATIONAL MEDITATIONS

Daily Prayer

I thank You Father God, that You are always with me and that You will never leave me nor forsake me. I pray to You, O Lord that my enemies will never triumph over me.

"Scripture for the Day"
Joshua Chapters 1-5

PHRASE OF THE DAY

The male is the source of the human family. This puts an awesome responsibility on the man as a husband and father. The male is the source, sustainer, nurturer, and protector of the female, because God took the woman out of the man. In society today too many women are doing the job of the man in the family, because too many men have abandonned their role in the family.

JANUARY 4TH

TRANSFORMATIONAL MEDITATIONS

"Scripture for the Day"
Psalm Chapters 1-2

PHRASE OF THE DAY

We are in charge of our lives and all of those who have been placed in our care, but God is in control. We don't know what the future holds, but we know who holds the future.

Daily Prayer

Lord, I ask that You forgive me for all my sins. Teach me Lord to walk in the path of righteousness and to delight in Your ways and to delight in Your word.

JANUARY 5TH

TRANSFORMATIONAL MEDITATIONS

Daily Prayer

Thank you Lord, for giving me another day and
another opportunity to stand on all of Your promises
O God. When the day comes that I shall be tested
and tried, help me O God to pass the test.

"Scripture for the Day"
Job Chapters 1-2

PHRASE OF THE DAY

The good news did not fit in the old religious system,
because it needed a fresh start. When you follow Christ,
look for new ways to look at people and new ways to
serve God. You can't put new wine in old wineskin.

JANUARY 6TH

TRANSFORMATIONAL MEDITATIONS

"Scripture for the Day"
Isaiah Chapters 1-6

PHRASE OF THE DAY

Our Father never coddles His children, the way we may spoil ours. He gives us success and joy, but every now and then He gives us a scolding behind the door. Thank Him.

Daily Prayer

Search my heart O God and remove and cleanse me from anything that does not look like You.

JANUARY 7TH

TRANSFORMATIONAL MEDITATIONS

Daily Prayer

Lord, help me to trust You, Your guidance and Your words. Help me, O Lord, to have faith even when I cannot see what's going on and do not understand where You are leading me.

"Scripture for the Day"
Matthew Chapters 1-2

PHRASE OF THE DAY

Jesus looks at you like a carpenter looks at a piece of wood; He sees what the wood will become. Full restoration is on the way, so hold on a little longer.

JANUARY 8TH

TRANSFORMATIONAL MEDITATIONS

"Scripture for the Day"
Romans Chapters 3-4

PHRASE OF THE DAY

How to navigate your way through life: first check your source of wisdom, then check your motive, last monitor your progress. Have a blessed day; encourage someone.

Daily Prayer

Lord, help me not to be caught up in religious acts and rituals, but to be caught up in You.

JANUARY 9TH

TRANSFORMATIONAL MEDITATIONS

Daily Prayer

O God, have mercy on the world we live in Lord.
Use me as an instrument to show Your love.

"Scripture for the Day"
Genesis Chapters 4-7

PHRASE OF THE DAY

What we feed our mind is just as important as what we
feed our body. Stand on the Word and watch the Lord raise
you above your situation. Shout, *"Thank you Lord!"*

JANUARY 10TH

TRANSFORMATIONAL MEDITATIONS

"Scripture for the Day"
Joshua Chapters 6-10

PHRASE OF THE DAY

Compassion is the greatest image of Abba; it comes from the Father and is placed in us. It grows when we let it flow on those who are hurting. Help someone today, Amen.

Daily Prayer

Lord, help me to obey You no matter how peculiar
Your instructions may seem. Help me Lord
not to be afraid, but to stand strong, even when
things seem like they are not in my favor.

JANUARY 11TH

TRANSFORMATIONAL MEDITATIONS

Daily Prayer

Lord, thank You for being a shield around me, protecting me from my enemies. I thank You also Lord for always hearing my prayers and my heart's cry. Surround me continuously with Your peace Father as I continuously stand in faith, trusting that You are always watching over me and my loved ones.

"Scripture for the Day"
Psalm Chapters 3-5

PHRASE OF THE DAY

Pride is the foundation of sin. Humility leads to Christ.

JANUARY 12TH

TRANSFORMATIONAL MEDITATIONS

"Scripture for the Day"
Job Chapters 3-4

PHRASE OF THE DAY

You become like who you are partnered with, so choose
your inner circle wisely. Choose those who will add value to
you and will benefit from you, improving every meeting.

Daily Prayer

Lord help me to praise You anyhow, even in the
midst of all of my circumstances. I give You all my
troubles, and I cast and lay at Your feet all of my
cares. Help me to sleep knowing without a shadow
of a doubt, that all is well, in Jesus' name, Amen.

JANUARY 13TH

TRANSFORMATIONAL MEDITATIONS

Daily Prayer

Pray a prayer pertaining to the scripture
passages found in Matthew Chapter 16.

For example: "Lord, give me wisdom, that I may know
the truth. Open my heart and my mind and my spirit
that I will know what is of You and what isn't."

"Scripture for the Day"
Isaiah Chapters 7-11

PHRASE OF THE DAY

Jesus sent the church into the world to be a reflection of
Himself. People are not coming to Christ because of our
poor image of Christ. Put down your own agenda.

JANUARY 14TH

TRANSFORMATIONAL MEDITATIONS

"Scripture for the Day"
Matthew Chapters 3-4

PHRASE OF THE DAY

When God sends a prophet into your land and immorality
is uncovered, humble yourself, repent, pray and watch
God heal your land. Thank God for His messenger.

Daily Prayer

Lord, help me to not allow my heart to ever be troubled,
and to never allow it to be afraid. I will lay my head
down in peace knowing that You alone are God and
nothing and no one is more powerful than You!

JANUARY 15TH

TRANSFORMATIONAL MEDITATIONS

Daily Prayer

Lord, have Your way in me.

"Scripture for the Day"
Romans Chapters 5-6

PHRASE OF THE DAY

Our work is to cast care; God's work is to take care!

JANUARY 16TH

TRANSFORMATIONAL MEDITATIONS

"Scripture for the Day"
Genesis Chapters 8-11

PHRASE OF THE DAY

Before you can help someone get to where they NEED to go, first help them see their present situation. Teach a just person and their knowledge will increase.

Daily Prayer

Lord, I thank You for all that You have done for me and for all that You have given both me and my family. Teach me Lord, how to honor, worship and bring glory to Your name with my talents and abilities.

JANUARY 17TH

TRANSFORMATIONAL MEDITATIONS

Daily Prayer

God, it is in You that I put my trust. Thank You, Lord, for handling my enemies. I will not fear, I will not be afraid.

"Scripture for the Day"
Joshua Chapters 11-15

PHRASE OF THE DAY

Nothing blesses a man more than being able to protect and care for his wife and children. Ladies, it hurts a man when he can't take care of you, if you have trust issues it hurts your man, even if he doesn't tell you. Men, if your wife came from a place where trust was broken, be patient in Jesus' name. Your words can help build or tear each other down.

JANUARY 18TH

TRANSFORMATIONAL MEDITATIONS

"Scripture for the Day"
Psalm Chapters 6-8

PHRASE OF THE DAY

This is the day that the Lord has made. Believers, the fight is beyond that of flesh and blood. Pick up thy shield of faith, go in the Spirit and take back what's yours.

Daily Prayer

Lord, if I have done anything that was not pleasing in Your sight, I ask that You forgive me Lord and cleanse me and make me whole. I repent of all my sins. Please Lord, forgive me for all my known and unknown sins and trespasses and help me to forgive those who have trespassed against me.

JANUARY 19TH

TRANSFORMATIONAL MEDITATIONS

Daily Prayer

Lord, in the midst of my trials and in the midst of my
tests, help me to speak words that both honor and glorify
You. Help me to always have praises on my lips and
to never doubt nor speak any evil against You.

"Scripture for the Day"
Job Chapters 5-6

PHRASE OF THE DAY

No salvation can ever come from the old covenant. Listen,
drop all trespasses made against you and ask for forgiveness of
the ones that you have made. Only God can change the heart.

JANUARY 20TH

TRANSFORMATIONAL MEDITATIONS

"Scripture for the Day"
Isaiah Chapters 12-17

PHRASE OF THE DAY

To keep ourselves from falling, we must refrain from emphasizing the gift of a leader over his or her character. This is a common and unhealthy tendency that can lead us astray.

Daily Prayer

Lord, help me not to despise correction, for Your Word says that You chasten those whom You love.

JANUARY 21ST

TRANSFORMATIONAL MEDITATIONS

Daily Prayer

Lord, help me to always see the light at the end of the tunnel. You are beautiful and You are wonderful, and I praise You this day. Cover me in Your precious blood Lord Jesus and keep me safe and out of harm's way.

"Scripture for the Day"
Matthew Chapters 5-7

PHRASE OF THE DAY

The man is God's security guard. When he shows up everyone is supposed to feel protected and safe. He is also supposed to teach about God's presence in his home and protect it. A woman should feel safe and secure around him. He should know that his purpose is to protect and guide her to God.

JANUARY 22ND

TRANSFORMATIONAL MEDITATIONS

"Scripture for the Day"
Romans Chapters 7-8

PHRASE OF THE DAY

Never give up! You can do ALL things when Christ is first
in your life. The more you study the Word the stronger
you will get; no pain no gain. Have a blessed day.

Daily Prayer

Thank You, Lord, for salvation and for setting us free! I
am no longer a slave to sin for I have been set free. Thank
You, Lord Jesus, for dying for me. I receive my freedom,
in Jesus' name and know that I am no longer condemned.

JANUARY 23RD

TRANSFORMATIONAL MEDITATIONS

Daily Prayer

Lord, help me not to pair up or be unequally yoked with anyone that you have not chosen to be a part of my journey nor have selected to be a part of my life. Remove all the Lots from my life Lord Jesus and give me a new name.

"Scripture for the Day"
Genesis Chapters 12-15

PHRASE OF THE DAY

1 Corinthians 13:7-8 teaches us that love bears all things, believes all things, hopes all things, endures all things, and that love never fails. Love does not keep score of faults and love is not selfish.

JANUARY 24TH

TRANSFORMATIONAL MEDITATIONS

"Scripture for the Day"
Joshua Chapters 16-20

PHRASE OF THE DAY

The enemy comes to steal, kill, and destroy, but he can only do that if you are in agreement with him. So, if you are addicted to anything, in sexual immorality, or ill, come out of agreement and repent. God is waiting for you.

Daily Prayer

O God, You are such a merciful and forgiving God. Thank You for making a way out of no way for Your people, for Your saints.

JANUARY 25TH

TRANSFORMATIONAL MEDITATIONS

Daily Prayer

I thank You this morning God, that all of my enemies will fall into the same traps that they have laid out and set before me. I do have the victory in Jesus' name.

"Scripture for the Day"
Psalm Chapters 9-11

PHRASE OF THE DAY

Hey believers, man was given work before woman was created. This means that before a man needs a woman, and before he is ready for marriage, he needs work. He needs to find out what God is calling him to do. Then use that vocation and work to take care of his future wife and children. A woman is supposed to marry someone who is already able to provide.

JANUARY 26TH

TRANSFORMATIONAL MEDITATIONS

"Scripture for the Day"
Job Chapters 7-8

PHRASE OF THE DAY

A true leader is a servant. They are not rulers. They take
care of others before themselves. Whoever wants to
become a great leader must know how to be a servant.

Daily Prayer

Lord, no matter how difficult and challenging at times life may
get, help me not to ever grow weary O Lord, and help me not
to ever faint. Grant me strength O God in the areas where I
am weak and help me Lord to forever love and trust in You.

JANUARY 27TH

TRANSFORMATIONAL MEDITATIONS

Daily Prayer

O God, protect Your people Lord from all that's going on in the world around us. Cover us in Your precious, precious blood. Protect us from all sickness and infirmities and keep our homes free from all forms of trouble and diseases.

"Scripture for the Day"
Isaiah Chapters 18-22

PHRASE OF THE DAY

To have authority means to have the right to govern. If a man is abusive towards his wife and kids and/or sleeps around, that is abuse of authority. Whenever you abuse your power, you lose legitimate authority. A man's strength lies not in his muscles, but in his spirit; meekness is power under control.

JANUARY 28TH

TRANSFORMATIONAL MEDITATIONS

"Scripture for the Day"
Matthew Chapters 8-10

PHRASE OF THE DAY

Music is a vehicle used to get close in the spirit, your destination depends on what bus you get on. Life and death are in the power of the tongue. So, the lyrics play a big part on what spirit you are getting close to. Think about it, do you want to help someone or injure someone while riding on your bus. If you get on the wrong bus and feel like hurting or disrespecting someone, then you need to transfer to the right bus.

Daily Prayer

O Lord, I believe in miracles, work Your wonderful miraculous miracles through me.

JANUARY 29ᵀᴴ

TRANSFORMATIONAL MEDITATIONS

Daily Prayer

Thank You, Lord, for saving me. Let me not be a disobedient individual, but rather be one who celebrates Your commands and follows Your voice and Your instructions. I bless Your Holy and Righteous name Lord Jesus. In Jesus' name, amen.

"Scripture for the Day"
Romans Chapters 9-10

PHRASE OF THE DAY

The Spirit of the Lord spoke two words to me for the body of Christ, weary and worry. He gave me the scripture Mark 4:18 NKJV, "*Now these are the ones sown among thorns; they are the ones who hear the word and the cares of the world, the deceitfulness of riches, and the desires for other things entering in choke the word and it became unfruitful.*" Trust in the Lord and lean not on anything else.

JANUARY 30TH

TRANSFORMATIONAL MEDITATIONS

"Scripture for the Day"
Genesis Chapters 16-19

PHRASE OF THE DAY

Remember when we were young and our parents took care of us, if we asked for something the burden to produce it was on our parents. God is the same way; we must be in good standing and ready to receive what we are asking for.

Daily Prayer

Lord, help me to give You the very best of me. O Lord help me to want to give You all of me.

JANUARY 31ST

TRANSFORMATIONAL MEDITATIONS

Daily Prayer

Dear Father, thank you for waking me up today. I come humbly before Your throne of Grace and Mercy asking God that You help me to continuously walk upright before You. Help me Lord to serve You in spirit and in truth and with everything within me.

"Scripture for the Day"
Joshua Chapters 21-24

PHRASE OF THE DAY

Let me tell you believers something, it does matter who you believe you are and not who people say you are. You are the salt of the earth, you are a child of God, and you are God's workmanship. You are also the temple of the Holy Spirit, and a new creation in Christ Jesus. Now start acting like who you are because of the Blood of Jesus. Your greatest enemy is doubt.

FEBRUARY 1ST

TRANSFORMATIONAL MEDITATIONS

"Scripture for the Day"
Psalm Chapters 12-14

PHRASE OF THE DAY

We were built to last and stand all tests. We must renew our mind with the Word of God and reflect. The enemy brings a constant dip of fear and doubt, only the Word of God can cast that out. Grace and mercy follow us all the days of our lives when you are a believer.

Daily Prayer

O Lord, help me to love no one, and nothing more than I love You. It is my wish and my sincere desire Lord, that my life, my words and my ways be pleasing to You.

FEBRUARY 2ND

TRANSFORMATIONAL MEDITATIONS

Daily Prayer

Help me Lord to remember in the midst of my trials,
my pain and my suffering that You see all, You know
all and that all things will work for my good.

"Scripture for the Day"
Job Chapters 9-10

PHRASE OF THE DAY

Bitterness is unfulfilled revenge. It is produced when
revenge is not satisfied to the degree we desire. Bitterness
is a root. If roots are nourished, watered, protected, fed, and
given attention, then they increase in depth and strength.
If not dealt with quickly, roots are hard to pull up.

FEBRUARY 3RD

TRANSFORMATIONAL MEDITATIONS

"Scripture for the Day"
Isaiah Chapters 23-28

PHRASE OF THE DAY

Like a good neighbor Jesus is there, with restoration.

Daily Prayer

Lord, it is in You that I live. It is in You that I breathe.
It is in You that I have my being. What a mighty and
faithful God I serve. Thank You, God, for all that
You have already done, in Jesus' name, Amen.

FEBRUARY 4TH

TRANSFORMATIONAL MEDITATIONS

Daily Prayer

Lord, I ask that You grant me wisdom, to know
what to say, when I am confronted and challenged
by those who really don't know who You are.

"Scripture for the Day"
Matthew Chapters 11-13

PHRASE OF THE DAY

Communication is one of the most important factors
in a relationship. Whether that relationship is between
man and God, parent and child, man and woman,
your family, friends or coworkers. Ask God to grant
you wisdom to communicate truth and positivity
with Him and towards those in our daily lives.

FEBRUARY 5ᵀᴴ

TRANSFORMATIONAL MEDITATIONS

"Scripture for the Day"
Romans Chapters 11-12

PHRASE OF THE DAY

Beware of false prophets and teachers, who come to you in sheep's clothing, but inwardly are ravenous wolves. You will know them by their fruit. Good trees bare good fruit and bad trees bare bad fruit.

Daily Prayer

Lord, I offer my body to You this day as a living sacrifice. Continue to help me daily Lord, to live holy and to live a life that is pleasing to You.

FEBRUARY 6TH

TRANSFORMATIONAL MEDITATIONS

Daily Prayer

Lord, help me to hold on to all of Your promises O
God, for You are a God who is a promise keeper and
Your Word will never return unto You void.

"Scripture for the Day"
Genesis Chapters 20-23

PHRASE OF THE DAY

Wisdom will save you from evil people and from those
who twist the truth. Stay clear from those who turn
from the right way to walk down dark paths. They take
pleasure in doing wrong, and they enjoy the twisted
ways of evil. If you are a believer and you go out
your way to associate with the character of the above;
remember that light and darkness cannot coexist.

FEBRUARY 7TH

TRANSFORMATIONAL MEDITATIONS

"Scripture for the Day"
Judges Chapters 1-6

PHRASE OF THE DAY

If a person does not have a relationship with God, they cannot fully function in their purpose. Hence, the helpmate is not right (overworked). Life and death are in the power of the tongue and we will eat the fruit of what we speak. So, I command your true purpose to rise up and have dominion in Jesus' name.

Daily Prayer

I thank you Lord that my enemies have already been defeated. Help me to continuously stand on Your promises.

FEBRUARY 8TH

TRANSFORMATIONAL MEDITATIONS

Daily Prayer

Lord, help me to obey all of Your commands,
that I may never be shaken.

"Scripture for the Day"
Psalm Chapters 15-17

PHRASE OF THE DAY

Nature or nurture, it doesn't matter, I know what's in
you from your outward expression. We need to reboot
our CPU, garbage in garbage out. The enemy is always
trying to infect us. The antivirus is Jesus. A scripture
a day, keeps the virus at bay. Exercise what you know
that is true and grow. Learn something new everyday,
which helps to prune and makes more room.

FEBRUARY 9TH

TRANSFORMATIONAL MEDITATIONS

"Scripture for the Day"
Job Chapters 11-12

PHRASE OF THE DAY

We cannot always choose what happens to us, but we can
choose our attitude towards each situation. The secret to
a cheerful heart is filling our minds with thoughts that are
true, pure, and loving. Train your mind to dwell on the good
things in life. Your altitude is measured by your attitude.

Daily Prayer

Lord in the midst of my trials and my tests, help my heart to
never grow bitter, but to still love and trust and worship You.

FEBRUARY 10TH

TRANSFORMATIONAL MEDITATIONS

Daily Prayer

Help me Lord to turn the other cheek and to
walk in love knowing that the battle is not
mine, but it belongs to You O Lord.

"Scripture for the Day"
Isaiah Chapters 29-33

PHRASE OF THE DAY

When people are not doing well, there is a tendency
to blame others. If faith comes from hearing the Word
of God, then fear comes from hearing the word of the
world (enemy). How will they hear less you preach
the good news? Please don't get weary in well doing,
for your good deeds will surely outshine evil.

FEBRUARY 11TH

TRANSFORMATIONAL MEDITATIONS

"Scripture for the Day"
Matthew Chapters 14-16

PHRASE OF THE DAY

I am convinced that neither: death nor life, nor angels nor demons, nor the present, nor future, nor height, nor depth, nor any power, nor any principality, nor anything bothering you today, nor anything else in all creation will be able to separate us from the love of God that is in Christ Jesus our Lord.

Daily Prayer

Lord, help me to not get swept up and enticed by the things of this world. Help me to crucify my flesh daily and serve You and only You. Help me to not make promises hastily, but to be of a sober mind in Christ Jesus, Amen.

FEBRUARY 12TH

TRANSFORMATIONAL MEDITATIONS

Daily Prayer

Lord, help me to honor what You honor and help me to respect
that which You respect this day and forevermore, Amen.

"Scripture for the Day"
Romans Chapters 13-14

PHRASE OF THE DAY

If God is for us, who can be against us? He who did not spare
His own Son, but gave Him up for US ALL, how would He
not also, along with Him, graciously give us all things?

FEBRUARY 13TH

TRANSFORMATIONAL MEDITATIONS

"Scripture for the Day"
Genesis Chapters 24-27

PHRASE OF THE DAY

The ungodly flee when God chastens them,
but believers kiss the chastening rod.

Daily Prayer

Help me God to consistently obey Your Word and
to know that as You did for Abraham, You will do
for me also; and my seed will be blessed.

FEBRUARY 14TH

TRANSFORMATIONAL MEDITATIONS

Daily Prayer

Heavenly Father show me how to feed my faith and
how to cast down all imaginations that rise up in my
thinking and that go contrary to Your Word. I love
You Lord. Please help me to trust You even more so
that I am never afraid. There is no fear in love.

"Scripture for the Day"
Judges Chapters 7-11

PHRASE OF THE DAY

Doubt is the weapon of the enemy, when you resist doubt,
faith increases. I pray your faith removes the blinders,
so you can see who you really are in the spirit.

FEBRUARY 15TH

TRANSFORMATIONAL MEDITATIONS

"Scripture for the Day"
Psalm Chapters 18-20

PHRASE OF THE DAY

Discernment is a gift from God that most people don't like, especially Christians that are not doing right when they are not in plain sight. Discernment can even expose who you are hanging around. Discernment is the gift that would expose the wolf in sheep's clothing. I pray for the increase of discernment in the true believers, in Jesus' name.

Daily Prayer

O God, thank you for always hearing my prayers. Give me my hearts desires O God as I continue to worship You. Let my will line up with Your will in Jesus' name.

FEBRUARY 16TH

TRANSFORMATIONAL MEDITATIONS

Daily Prayer

O Heavenly Father, help me to speak good and not evil in the midst of all my trials, my tribulations and in the midst of all of my circumstances. Help me to always have praises on my lips and glorify Your name.

"Scripture for the Day"
Job Chapters 13-14

PHRASE OF THE DAY

The truth is your purpose for living, which is inside you from birth. Lack of knowledge WILL lead you away from your purpose. Seek understanding from the Lord thy God.

FEBRUARY 17TH

TRANSFORMATIONAL MEDITATIONS

"Scripture for the Day"
Isaiah Chapters 34-39

PHRASE OF THE DAY

I thank all those prayer warriors that get up in the middle
of the night and wage war in prayer for our nation. I am a
retired soldier, so I know what it takes to protect a nation
without a thank you sometimes. Well, the Spirit of the Lord
is prompting me to say thank you. I pray for your families
and for all of those whom you are steward over. I plead the
Blood of Jesus over all of you saints, in Jesus' name, Amen.

Daily Prayer

Lord, help me to let go. Teach me how to have peace
in the midst of the storm. I release all my enemies
to You Father, right now, for Your Word says that
vengeance is Yours, and that You shall repay.

FEBRUARY 18TH

TRANSFORMATIONAL MEDITATIONS

Daily Prayer

Heavenly Father and my God! I am so thankful that You are still in the miracle working business, for You are a God who heals. Touch me and my loved ones today Father and heal every sickness, every illness, and every wound.

"Scripture for the Day"
Matthew Chapters 17-19

PHRASE OF THE DAY

The Word says don't get weary in well doing, that means we will get weary. No one said this work would be easy, so we need to help each other out. The problem is not the world but the saints attacking each other. Who was it that brought Jesus to the cross? I pray that the body stops all self-inflicted wounds and use their gifts that were given freely to build up the body for His kingdom's sake.

FEBRUARY 19TH

TRANSFORMATIONAL MEDITATIONS

"Scripture for the Day"
Romans Chapters 15-16

PHRASE OF THE DAY

If you are a believer, may no weapon formed against
you prosper, and every tongue that rises against you
in judgment be condemned. In Jesus' name.

Daily Prayer

Lord, help me not to be selfish, but to walk in love and to be
prepared to always be there to lend a helping hand to those
all around me who might be going through some sort of
difficulty. Give me the words to say, O Lord, so that I may be
of some comfort and strength to their lives and to their hearts.

FEBRUARY 20TH

TRANSFORMATIONAL MEDITATIONS

Daily Prayer

God, help me to be obedient, especially when
I don't understand. For Your Word is true and
You know what's best for my life.

"Scripture for the Day"
Genesis Chapters 28-31

PHRASE OF THE DAY

God is so good to us that He doesn't give us more than we
can handle. Many of us want everything now. Be patient, for
God is developing your character to be able to handle more.

FEBRUARY 21ST

TRANSFORMATIONAL MEDITATIONS

"Scripture for the Day"
Judges Chapters 12-16

PHRASE OF THE DAY

If there is a contest between you and God, I pick God to win. God created us for a purpose and we can change it. For example, He created men and women with a purpose to be fruitful and multiply, but we have some going against their purpose. When we go against our purpose, you best believe Satan is involved. If God said you're going to preach, teach, or prophesy, then I pray that you will submit.

Daily Prayer

Lord, I believe but help my unbelief in every area of my life, where faith is lacking, that I may trust in Your Word, without a shadow of a doubt.

FEBRUARY 22ND

TRANSFORMATIONAL MEDITATIONS

Daily Prayer

Father God, today, I just want to say thank you. I
thank You Lord that Your love never fails.

"Scripture for the Day"
Psalm Chapters 21-23

PHRASE OF THE DAY

Atonement is the brain and spinal cord of salvation. Take
away the cleansing blood, and what is left for the guilty?
Deny the substitution of Jesus for us and you have denied all
that is precious in the New Testament. Never let us endure
one waving doubtful thought about this all-important truth.

FEBRUARY 23RD

TRANSFORMATIONAL MEDITATIONS

"Scripture for the Day"
Job Chapters 15-16

PHRASE OF THE DAY

Whenever you are trouble shooting anything electrical, start with the simplest thing first by checking the plug. Well, it works the same way with God. First, are you truly connected? This obvious oversight is normally the problem; plug yourself back into God.

Daily Prayer

Lord, Your Word says that if any man lacks wisdom, let him ask. O God, grant me more wisdom today. In Jesus' name, amen, amen and amen. Thank You Lord.

FEBRUARY 24TH

TRANSFORMATIONAL MEDITATIONS

Daily Prayer

I thank You Lord that my sins are forgiven; past, present
and future. Lord, today I ask that You continue to help me
to sin less each and every single day. I want my life to be
pleasing to You Lord. I surrender all, in Jesus' name, Amen.

"Scripture for the Day"
Isaiah Chapters 40-44

PHRASE OF THE DAY

Excuses are everywhere excellence is not. If you seek
excellence, you must avoid the bad habit of excuses.
Whatever your job is, it is up to you to master your craft.
Rationalization, it's what we do when we substitute false
explanations for true reasons. It is also when we cloud our
actual motives with a smoke screen of nice sounding excuses.

FEBRUARY 25TH

TRANSFORMATIONAL MEDITATIONS

"Scripture for the Day"
Matthew Chapters 20-22

PHRASE OF THE DAY

We need to come to terms that we have to deal with two issues
until we meet the Father, which is that we are both kings and
slaves, for we feel His presence and the pressures of sin.

Daily Prayer

God, help me not to stand idle, but to be productive
in the right things each and every single day O
Lord. Help me to be productive in You.

FEBRUARY 26TH

TRANSFORMATIONAL MEDITATIONS

Daily Prayer

Father God, today I lift up the body of Christ. God, help us to be united and to function as a team and as one body, serving you in spirit and in truth, in Jesus' name, Amen.

"Scripture for the Day"
1st Corinthians Chapters 1-2

PHRASE OF THE DAY

It is scientifically easier to pull down than it is to push up. For this reason, it is better to surround yourself, which is your job, with people who lift up and encourage on purpose. Remember it is easier to tear others down. Use your gift to build up the Kingdom of God.

FEBRUARY 27TH

TRANSFORMATIONAL MEDITATIONS

"Scripture for the Day"
Genesis Chapters 32-35

PHRASE OF THE DAY

This world was made for you and you are very special
to God. Sometimes we overlook that truth. Encourage
someone today as well as yourself, through Jesus' name.

Daily Prayer

O God, I thank You for sending Your angels to stand guard
and to watch over me. Show me how to use them Lord and
to dispatch them all around me to fight against the enemy.

FEBRUARY 28TH

TRANSFORMATIONAL MEDITATIONS

Daily Prayer

O God tear down every idol that I have built, both in
my heart and in my mind. Forgive me Father for ever
putting anyone or anything in Your place and above You.
I repent this day and ask that You lead and guide me and
help me to always put You first. In Jesus' name, amen.

"Scripture for the Day"
Judges Chapters 17-19

PHRASE OF THE DAY

What is the difference between Grace (Spirit) and works
(flesh)? Let's look at Abraham with his son's Isaac (Spirit) and
Ishmael (works). God's Grace produced Isaac and Abraham's
works made Ishmael. If God promised you something, then
His Grace is sufficient and doesn't need your works. You
just need to work the faith that He issued you. Put your
Ishmael down and believe in God's Grace, in Jesus' name.

FEBRUARY 29TH

TRANSFORMATIONAL MEDITATIONS

"Scripture for the Day"
Judges Chapters 20-21

PHRASE OF THE DAY

One of the greatest responsibilities of a parent is to encourage their children to become wise. If you want wisdom, you must decide to go after it. This takes determination not to abandon the search no matter what obstacles may arise. This is not a once in a lifetime step, but a daily process of choosing between two paths.

Daily Prayer

I thank you God that You have granted me victory over my enemies. As I lay my head to sleep, protect me also in my dreams.

MARCH 1ST

TRANSFORMATIONAL MEDITATIONS

Daily Prayer

Lord, help me to never forget that everything is in the palm of Your hands. For You are God and there is none like You.

"Scripture for the Day"
Psalm Chapters 24-26

PHRASE OF THE DAY

"God, grant me the serenity to accept the things I cannot change, courage to change the things I can, and wisdom to know the difference." Dr. Reinhold Niebuhr.

MARCH 2ND

TRANSFORMATIONAL MEDITATIONS

"Scripture for the Day"
Job Chapters 17-18

PHRASE OF THE DAY

You can be very sincere in your efforts to do something but if you don't know its purpose you will be sincerely wrong, i.e., marriage, work, children, relationship.

Daily Prayer

Lord, muzzle my mouth that I may never speak against You. For no matter what is going on in either my life or in the world, You are always worthy to be praised.

MARCH 3RD

TRANSFORMATIONAL MEDITATIONS

Daily Prayer

Father God, thank You for waking me up today
and for protecting me all night long as I slept. Use
me as an instrument to show others that You are
real God, so that they may believe in You.

"Scripture for the Day"
Isaiah Chapters 45-50

PHRASE OF THE DAY

You have not chosen God, but He has chosen and
ordained you, so that you may bring forth fruit. You
were purchased, with the blood of Jesus Christ.

MARCH 4TH

TRANSFORMATIONAL MEDITATIONS

"Scripture for the Day"
Matthew Chapters 23-25

PHRASE OF THE DAY

Hey men, we need to get to a place where we know God's presence. A place where we have a desire to work, are able to cultivate, and can protect everything in our care - family, community and church. A place where we know God's Word and are able to teach it to our family and community. A man of purpose knows who he is, where he is, and what he is supposed to be doing.

Daily Prayer

Lord, help me not to be hypocritical and self-righteous like the Pharisees, but rather peaceful and humble and continuously giving You praise.

MARCH 5TH

TRANSFORMATIONAL MEDITATIONS

Daily Prayer

My Lord, help me not to be a carnal Christian,
but to walk in the Spirit always.

"Scripture for the Day"
1st Corinthians Chapters 3-4

PHRASE OF THE DAY

God gave us His best and all He asks in return, is
for us to do the same. Jealousy caused Cain to lose
his way and kill his brother. Don't be like Cain and
give God a mess; work hard and do your best.

MARCH 6TH

TRANSFORMATIONAL MEDITATIONS

"Scripture for the Day"
Genesis Chapters 36-39

PHRASE OF THE DAY

A man's purpose is to cultivate, nurture, protect, and provide
for his family, neighborhood, and church. When one's purpose
is perverted, it destroys the fabric of our community.

Daily Prayer

Father God, please teach me and show me my Lord,
those who i can share my visions, my hopes, my
dreams and knowledge with; and those that I should
be silent with concerning all that You reveal to me.

MARCH 7TH

TRANSFORMATIONAL MEDITATIONS

Daily Prayer

Lord, please protect my family and I, in the midst of all
the trials and tribulations that will occur on this planet.
Help our faith not to fail, but to stand strong in the hour
that it is tested. In Jesus' name I ask these things. Amen.

"Scripture for the Day"
The Book of Ruth

PHRASE OF THE DAY

Ishmael was born by works and Isaac was born by
faith. Let God be in your life, stop trying to be God.

MARCH 8TH

TRANSFORMATIONAL MEDITATIONS

"Scripture for the Day"
Psalm Chapters 27-29

PHRASE OF THE DAY

Consider it a chance for growth when we are faced with trials, because of what it can produce in our lives, patience, character, and perseverance. Pressure brings out the real you.

Daily Prayer

I thank You God that You are a merciful God. I thank You for Your love, Your protection, Your peace, Your warmth and Your comfort, especially in the midst of the storm.

MARCH 9TH

TRANSFORMATIONAL MEDITATIONS

Daily Prayer

My Lord, let not my heart be troubled regarding the seeming prosperity of the wicked. For You see all, know all, hear all and are not blind to the sins of evil men. Lord, I release everyone in my life to You, trusting and knowing that vengeance is Yours and You will repay them for all their wicked deeds.

"Scripture for the Day"
Job Chapters 19-20

PHRASE OF THE DAY

The church is under attack by the false teachings, we need to look in the mirror and truthfully say what we see. The world retaliates, while the church leaves that task to God. The Word says pray for, feed, and give your enemy water to drink. Love is the message of the Lord, being believers we should resemble that message.

MARCH 10TH

TRANSFORMATIONAL MEDITATIONS

"Scripture for the Day"
Isaiah Chapters 51-55

PHRASE OF THE DAY

You were designed to bring out the very best in everything
that's in your care. You, are never given a finished work
by God, but you are given raw materials and resources.

Daily Prayer

Heavenly Father, I thank You for a spirit of joy. Help
me to desire to continuously offer You praise. Wake me
up in the morning O Lord, with a new song of worship
in my heart, that I may rejoice and sing to You.

MARCH 11TH

TRANSFORMATIONAL MEDITATIONS

Daily Prayer

God I thank You for being a miracle working God. You
are a God who heals. You are a God of miracles.

"Scripture for the Day"
Matthew Chapters 26-28

PHRASE OF THE DAY

A child in Christ could be from the ages of youth to grey,
but it depends on when they came to the Lord. The problem
we have in the body of Christ is the lack of training of our
children. So, when they go out to minister, they are equipped
with false teaching, which creates separation in the body.
Let's focus on His Word and use God as a compass to
guide and protect our family. Train up a child on the way
he should go, and when he is old, he will not turn from it.

MARCH 12TH

TRANSFORMATIONAL MEDITATIONS

"Scripture for the Day"
1st Corinthians Chapters 5-6

PHRASE OF THE DAY

Once man falls in love with Jesus's presence, that man begins to truly function. They will also find out that buried inside them is the work they have to do for God.

Daily Prayer

Heavenly Father, I thank You Lord for waking me up this morning and Lord I ask humbly that You allow me and help me to remember You throughout the day. Please continue to protect me and my loved ones, in Jesus' name I pray. Amen. Amen. Amen.

MARCH 13TH

TRANSFORMATIONAL MEDITATIONS

Daily Prayer

Dear Heavenly Father, please grant me more wisdom and give me also the ability to understand my visions and dreams.

"Scripture for the Day"
Genesis Chapters 40-43

PHRASE OF THE DAY

A grudge is one thing that doesn't get better when it's nursed. It gets worse.

MARCH 14TH

TRANSFORMATIONAL MEDITATIONS

"Scripture for the Day"
1st Samuel Chapters 1-5

PHRASE OF THE DAY

No man is justified by the law in the sight of God it is evident. For the just shall live by faith that Jesus already finished the work; we just have to believe.

Daily Prayer

My Lord, protect my life from all trickery. Let no one around me be deceived by the plots and the plans and the lies of the enemy.

MARCH 15TH

TRANSFORMATIONAL MEDITATIONS

Daily Prayer

O God, my God, in You I put my trust. Let my
trust in You never put me to shame, but rather
bring glory and honor to Your Holy name.

"Scripture for the Day"
Psalm Chapters 30-32

PHRASE OF THE DAY

Painful experiences can be a marvelous gateway to rich
fellowship as we bear each other's burdens. Remember
all things work for your good because you love God.

MARCH 16TH

TRANSFORMATIONAL MEDITATIONS

"Scripture for the Day"
Job Chapters 21-22

PHRASE OF THE DAY

If a man is going to love his wife like Christ loved the church and sanctified it, he is going to need to know Christ. To sanctify is to set apart and protect.

Daily Prayer

O Lord, let my life bring pleasure to Your heart and glorify Your name. I love You God; help me to love You even more.

MARCH 17TH

TRANSFORMATIONAL MEDITATIONS

Daily Prayer

Lord, help me not to run away from You, and from
What You have designed and created me to be. Help
me not to walk or run away from my calling, for it is
in You that I live and breathe and have my being.

"Scripture for the Day"
Isaiah Chapters 56-61

PHRASE OF THE DAY

When things are not working properly, we get help. If our
car breaks down, we take it to a mechanic. When we get
sick, we see a doctor. A/C breaks, we call a repairman. Yet
when it comes to a marriage not functioning properly, too
many say."O*h well, it will fix itself.*" or they just let it go.
What is our priority? Don't be afraid to ask God for help.

MARCH 18TH

TRANSFORMATIONAL MEDITATIONS

"Scripture for the Day"
Mark Chapters 1-2

PHRASE OF THE DAY

Husbands love your wives just as Christ loved the church and gave Himself for her. Husbands above all else, love your wife. Don't worry about anything else before that, all other things work out better when you are working together.

Daily Prayer

Dear Father, prepare me for the coming
of Your Son, Jesus Christ.

MARCH 19TH

TRANSFORMATIONAL MEDITATIONS

Daily Prayer

My Lord, help me to have self-control over
my body that I may not sin against You.

"Scripture for the Day"
1st Corinthians Chapters 7-8

PHRASE OF THE DAY

Shall broken hearts, drugs, unemployment, family, sickness,
finances, or any other created thing separate us from
the love of Christ? All things work out for our good.

MARCH 20TH

TRANSFORMATIONAL MEDITATIONS

"Scripture for the Day"
Genesis Chapters 44 - 47

PHRASE OF THE DAY

If you take a fish out of water and put it on the sidewalk, do you have to do anything else to kill it? No, because the fish is away from its source of life. We are affected in the same manner, if we are away from our source of life, like the fish, we will slowly perish. Our source of life is God.

Daily Prayer

O God, You know all things. In this life there are many things we don't understand. Please help me Lord to trust You even when things aren't looking up. When things are not looking in my favor, help me Lord to know that You always have a plan and a purpose for what You allow to happen here on Earth. I trust You Lord, please help my faith to increase.

MARCH 21ST

TRANSFORMATIONAL MEDITATIONS

Daily Prayer

O God touch my heart also, that I may serve You, and
prophesy, and be used as a messenger of the Word of
God by You. Help me O God to be able to stand and
to not only stand, but to stand strong and tall even in
the midst of my enemies. Let my light so shine that
when men see it, Your name will be glorified.

"Scripture for the Day"
1st Samuel Chapters 6-10

PHRASE OF THE DAY

Woe to those teachers who clean the outside of their cups,
but the inside is full of greed and self-indulgence. Blind
teachers first clean the inside of your cup, then the outside
will be clean. Avoid being like a washed tomb, clean on
the outside and on the inside full of dead men's bones.

MARCH 22ND

TRANSFORMATIONAL MEDITATIONS

"Scripture for the Day"
Psalm Chapters 33-35

PHRASE OF THE DAY

A woman is the receiver and a reflector. The man is the
giver. The Bible says husband love your wife. Wives
are instructed to honor, respect and submit to their
own husband. When a husband loves his wife, she will
reflect what she receives. Men you would be wise to
obey the Lord's counsel, it's for your own good.

Daily Prayer

Heavenly Father, as I lay my head down to sleep tonight,
I say thank You. I thank You and give You praise Father
God, that You are a God who keeps His promises. You are a
righteous God and You are also just and I give You praise.

MARCH 23RD

TRANSFORMATIONAL MEDITATIONS

Daily Prayer

Father God, no matter what is either going on in my
life or not happening, help my heart to not get bitter.
Help me Lord to trust You in spite of what I don't see
and what I do not understand. Everything You allow
is for a purpose, in Jesus' mighty name, amen.

"Scripture for the Day"
Job Chapters 23-24

PHRASE OF THE DAY

The same God who created life in you can be trusted with the
details of your life. God doesn't ignore who depends on Him.

MARCH 24TH

TRANSFORMATIONAL MEDITATIONS

"Scripture for the Day"
Isaiah Chapters 62-66

PHRASE OF THE DAY

Good teaching comes from good learning and Proverbs has a
lot to say to those who want to learn wisdom. Proverbs make
it clear that there is no alternative to learning good wisdom.
We either become wise learners or refuse to learn and become
foolish failures. A proverb a day keeps temptation at bay.

Daily Prayer

O God, let my life be a life that You rejoice over. Let my
thoughts be Your thoughts, and my ways be Your ways.
I desire to live a life that is pleasing in Your sight.

MARCH 25TH

TRANSFORMATIONAL MEDITATIONS

Daily Prayer

Lord, my Lord, help me not to fall into the trap of being religious. For I want to have a relationship with You.

"Scripture for the Day"
Mark Chapters 3-4

PHRASE OF THE DAY

Goshen means draw near. When God calls you to Goshen, God wants you to draw near to Him, so He can keep you while the world goes through famine. God's love will protect you and yours from the wiles of the enemy. Goshen is now a spirit place, and place of obedience.

MARCH 26TH

TRANSFORMATIONAL MEDITATIONS

"Scripture for the Day"
1st Corinthians Chapters 9-10

PHRASE OF THE DAY

Whatever breakthrough you are believing Jesus for, He
says to you "I AM WILLING." Don't doubt because
of your own rationalization and do not disqualify
or condemn yourself. Let Jesus love you.

Daily Prayer

Goodnight Lord, thank You for keeping me and getting
me through this day. O Lord, I ask that You help me to
not be overly concerned or bothered in the slightest bit
by what others think of me. Help me Lord, to be sensitive
only to Your Holy Spirit and to what You think of me.

MARCH 27TH

TRANSFORMATIONAL MEDITATIONS

Daily Prayer

My Lord, help me to completely surrender my will to
You. Father, I know that You know best. The world has
its ideas of what should happen and when they should
take place, but You Father God, You know best.

"Scripture for the Day"
Genesis Chapters 48-50

PHRASE OF THE DAY

Lord, help me not to sin, because Your Word
says that the wages of sin is death, but the gift of
God is eternal life in Christ Jesus our Lord.

MARCH 28TH

TRANSFORMATIONAL MEDITATIONS

"Scripture for the Day"
1st Samuel Chapters 11-15

PHRASE OF THE DAY

God did not intend for us to worry about anything. 1 Peter 5:7 says, *"Cast all your anxiety on him because he cares for you."*

Daily Prayer

Lord, help me not to ever forget where I came from. Lord, help me to remember all of my victories in You, that my heart may always be grateful and faithful to You.

MARCH 29TH

TRANSFORMATIONAL MEDITATIONS

Daily Prayer

Today O God, I humbly pray for my enemies. Turn their hearts O God towards You. I pray that they all come to the knowledge of Christ Jesus and that they will repent and be saved, in Jesus mighty name, amen.

"Scripture for the Day"
Psalm Chapters 36-38

PHRASE OF THE DAY

Get rid of your pride and come home.

MARCH 30TH

TRANSFORMATIONAL MEDITATIONS

"Scripture for the Day"
Job Chapters 25-26

PHRASE OF THE DAY

I read this question and I felt it deserved to be asked.
*"What is the difference between inviting Jesus to be
the Lord over your kingdom, and you entering the
Kingdom of God?"* Think well before you answer.

Daily Prayer

Father God, please grant me more wisdom Lord, and
help me to speak things that glorify You. Give me a
discerning spirt so that I may recognize the truth.

MARCH 31ST

TRANSFORMATIONAL MEDITATIONS

Daily Prayer

O God, help me never to turn my back on You. Help me Father God to know You and to serve You in spirit and in truth and to always magnify You.

"Scripture for the Day"
Jeremiah Chapters 1-6

PHRASE OF THE DAY

My cup has runneth over for the people complaining and asking, *"How could God let this or that happen?"* When we went prodigal and were having fun engaging in sin, it was not God who told us to drink, fornicate, lie, steal, nor to bring death towards us. We as a people need to take responsibility for our part and repent.

APRIL 1ST

TRANSFORMATIONAL MEDITATIONS

"Scripture for the Day"
Mark Chapters 5-6

PHRASE OF THE DAY

Lashing out at others is a sure sign that something is wrong with us. Don't let your hurt pride lead you to hurt others.

Daily Prayer

O Lord, work Your miracles, signs and wonders through me, so that men will see them and glorify You and be saved.

APRIL 2ND

TRANSFORMATIONAL MEDITATIONS

Daily Prayer

Father God, help me to discover and tap into all
of my spiritual gifts. Show me how to use them
properly to help to edify the body of Christ.

"Scripture for the Day"
1st Corinthians Chapters 11-12

PHRASE OF THE DAY

If someone has a contagious disease, it is not cruel to
quarantine that person so that they do not infect others.
Sin is contagious and we must keep those who we are
steward over from it with education and demonstration.

APRIL 3RD

TRANSFORMATIONAL MEDITATIONS

"Scripture for the Day"
Exodus Chapters 1-4

PHRASE OF THE DAY

Sin allows Satan to come into your life to steal, kill, and destroy. You are a new creature in Christ Jesus, put sinful ways behind you, do not give it a foothold.

Daily Prayer

Lord, grant me the courage to do all the things that You have called me to do. Help me to never question my calling Lord. Help me to walk boldly, knowing that whatever You have called me to do, I am able to do with You. You are not a God of mistakes, but rather a God who fulfills His promises. In Jesus name, amen.

APRIL 4TH

TRANSFORMATIONAL MEDITATIONS

Daily Prayer

Lord, this morning I ask that You give me the strength and the grace to let the past be the past and to simply move forward. Help me to take it just one day at a time, in Jesus' name, Amen.

"Scripture for the Day"
1st Samuel Chapters 16-20

PHRASE OF THE DAY

"May the God of hope fill you with all joy and peace as you trust in Him, so that you may overflow with hope by the power of the Holy Spirt."

Romans 15:13

APRIL 5TH

TRANSFORMATIONAL MEDITATIONS

"Scripture for the Day"
Psalm Chapters 39-41

PHRASE OF THE DAY

A lot of believers still are thinking the way the world thinks.
Instead of going to the Word they go to other things. Be
transformed, by renewing your mind with the Word.

Daily Prayer

Thank You, God, for always hearing my cry. Thank
You for always coming to my rescue when I call upon
Your name. You are such a great and marvelous God.
Tonight Lord, I just want to give You praise.

APRIL 6TH

TRANSFORMATIONAL MEDITATIONS

Daily Prayer

God, help me not to entertain meaningless talk. Allow me to see clearly who is a friend and who is an enemy.

"Scripture for the Day"
Job Chapters 27-28

PHRASE OF THE DAY

You should have someone speaking positivity in your life. When you feel bad or have pains, you should be able to call someone to speak death to your pains and mood and speak life to your thinking. Most people think and speak themselves into the hospital.

APRIL 7TH

TRANSFORMATIONAL MEDITATIONS

"Scripture for the Day"
Jeremiah Chapters 7-11

PHRASE OF THE DAY

"Take my yoke upon you and learn from me, for I am gentle and humble in heart, and you will find rest for your souls." Matthew 11:29

Daily Prayer

Father God, help me to have a heart like David. One that will confess all its sins to You and repent and be ruthlessly honest with You. Let me not be wise in my own eyes, but rather be humble.

APRIL 8TH

TRANSFORMATIONAL MEDITATIONS

Daily Prayer

Lord, help me not to be religious like the Pharisees
who focus on the outward appearance of man.
Help me to judge wisely and to have a spirit of
discernment to decipher what is the real truth.

"Scripture for the Day"
Mark Chapters 7-8

PHRASE OF THE DAY

You don't become a soldier by just wearing the uniform;
it takes training (experience). Standing on the Word of
God through the storm or fire, produces soldiers.

APRIL 9TH

TRANSFORMATIONAL MEDITATIONS

"Scripture for the Day"
1st Corinthians Chapters 13-14

PHRASE OF THE DAY

God's Word is true and holds many promises for not only our life here on Earth, but also for our life, thereafter in Heaven. *"Very truly I tell you, whoever hears my word and believes Him who sent me has eternal life and will not be judged but has crossed over from death to life".* John 5:24

Daily Prayer

Lord, help me to walk in love and not to complain.

APRIL 10TH

TRANSFORMATIONAL MEDITATIONS

Daily Prayer

Lord, help me to understand that the flesh will never understand the things of the Spirit, and to know that they are always at war. Help me to be mindful to walk in the Spirit and to not entertain the things of the flesh.

"Scripture for the Day"
Exodus Chapters 5-8

PHRASE OF THE DAY

Repay no evil with evil. Have regard for all good things in the sight of all men. Strive to live peacefully with all men. Beloved, do not avenge yourself, but rather give up the position of wrath. For, *"Vengeance is mine…"*
says the Lord.

APRIL 11TH

TRANSFORMATIONAL MEDITATIONS

"Scripture for the Day"
1st Samuel Chapters 21-25

PHRASE OF THE DAY

Wherever you find faith, you will see God's presence.
God does not dwell where there is unbelief. We walk by
faith and not by sight. Seek His face daily and watch.

Daily Prayer

Heavenly Father, give me both the courage and the strength to
be who, and how, and what You created me to be. I need Your
help Lord, to truly love myself for who and what I am created
to be and to not try to be like anyone or
anything else.

APRIL 12TH

TRANSFORMATIONAL MEDITATIONS

Daily Prayer

O God, be my guiding light in the times of confusion, heartache, pain and darkness. Guide me through the wilderness and help me to put my trust in You.

"Scripture for the Day"
Psalm Chapters 42-44

PHRASE OF THE DAY

Don't be discouraged for Satan will blow and yell, but rest assured there is nothing he can do to stop you; providing that you continue to trust the Lord.

APRIL 13TH

TRANSFORMATIONAL MEDITATIONS

"Scripture for the Day"
Job Chapters 29-30

PHRASE OF THE DAY

Do we really understand what was accomplished in Jesus' life and death on the cross? He did more than just die for our sins. *"But he was pierced for our transgressions, he was crushed for our iniquities, the punishment that brought us peace was on him, and by his wound we are healed."* Isaiah 53:5

Meditate on this scripture throughout the day and ask God to give you a deeper revelation on what it *really* means.

Jesus died, so that we may truly have peace and live in freedom.

Daily Prayer

O God, teach me my Lord how to be more intimate with You. I want to be closer to You.

APRIL 14TH

TRANSFORMATIONAL MEDITATIONS

Daily Prayer

O Lord, help me to be consistently obedient to You. Let me not be like the wicked who are stubborn and refuse to listen to You.

"Scripture for the Day"
Jeremiah Chapters 12-16

PHRASE OF THE DAY

There is always a distance between the promise and the possession, and that distance is never uneventful, but it is designed to build your faith in God.

APRIL 15TH

TRANSFORMATIONAL MEDITATIONS

"Scripture for the Day"
Mark Chapters 9-10

PHRASE OF THE DAY

Don't be a believer in name only; your
life must bear good fruit.

Daily Prayer

Goodnight Father God. My prayer this night is that You
help me to clearly see the areas and the people in my
life that are stumbling blocks. Then, by Your grace and
mercy Lord, help me to cut them off. Help me not to
want anything that hinders my relationship with You.

APRIL 16TH

TRANSFORMATIONAL MEDITATIONS

Daily Prayer

O Lord, my God, my Heavenly Father, God of Heaven and Earth. In our modern days, whenever the time comes for You to make a distinction between those who are Israelites and those who are pagans, let me be on Israel's side.

"Scripture for the Day"
1st Corinthians Chapters 15-16

PHRASE OF THE DAY

All authority in Heaven and Earth has been given to You through Jesus.

Go make disciples of all, baptizing them in the name of the Father, Son, and Holy Spirit.

APRIL 17TH

TRANSFORMATIONAL MEDITATIONS

"Scripture for the Day"
Exodus Chapters 9-12

PHRASE OF THE DAY

When your mind starts being renewed after salvation, everyone should see the light on you and the shadows falling away. Keep seeking the face of the Father.

Daily Prayer

O Lord, have mercy on those who will not listen to You, and keep Your promises to those who do listen.

APRIL 18TH

TRANSFORMATIONAL MEDITATIONS

Daily Prayer

O Lord, help me not to take revenge on my enemies.
Give me the strength to say no to any evil desire that
presents itself to me, and to remember that vengeance
belongs to you. You O Lord, shall repay my enemies.

"Scripture for the Day"
1st Samuel Chapters 26-31

PHRASE OF THE DAY

It's not the will of the Father for any man or woman to live
in regret. There is nothing you can do about the past. Clean
up what you can, ask for forgiveness and let the grace of
the Father do the rest. If the Son therefore shall make you
free, you shall be free indeed. If you agree say Amen.

APRIL 19TH

TRANSFORMATIONAL MEDITATIONS

"Scripture for the Day"
Psalm Chapters 45-47

PHRASE OF THE DAY

Frustration is a feeling of dissatisfaction and also a form of deception. People are all different, so if you expect them to react the way you would, you are not being realistic and frustration will set in. Give to others, by satisfying their needs the way they want it, this will bring true fulfillment.

Daily Prayer

Tonight, O Lord, I give You praise. I say thank You Lord, for what You have already done. For You alone are worthy to be praised. I will make a joyful noise unto the Lord. Unto the Lord, I will shout Praise!

APRIL 20TH

TRANSFORMATIONAL MEDITATIONS

Daily Prayer

Lord, deliver me from a spirit of lust, that I may not be
lured away by anything considered as sinful gain.

"Scripture for the Day"
Job Chapters 31-32

PHRASE OF THE DAY

The enemy has always been against family. Whatever
your difference, make peace. To keep strife is self-
destruction. Praise God for restoration.

APRIL 21ST

TRANSFORMATIONAL MEDITATIONS

"Scripture for the Day"
Jeremiah Chapters 17-21

PHRASE OF THE DAY

Most believers are at the foot of the cross, where they received the grace gift of salvation. That road leads behind the cross where true love and forgiveness are. *"If someone says, "I love God," but hates a fellow believer, that person is a liar; for if we don't love people we can see, how can we love God, whom we cannot see?"* 1 John 4:20. Love your enemies. I'll see you behind the cross.

Daily Prayer

Father God, help me to boldly speak and proclaim the Word of the Lord, despite whatever attacks and persecutions I may face from my enemies and from the world.

APRIL 22ND

TRANSFORMATIONAL MEDITATIONS

Daily Prayer

Lord, Your words never cease to amaze me. Grant me more wisdom Lord, so that my words may be Your words and bring glory to Your name.

"Scripture for the Day"
Mark Chapters 11-12

PHRASE OF THE DAY

When you repent something has to been done, restitution. This is when you try to make right a wrong you have committed. This process transforms you, preventing you from doing that act again.

APRIL 23RD

TRANSFORMATIONAL MEDITATIONS

"Scripture for the Day"
2nd Corinthians Chapters 1-3

PHRASE OF THE DAY

Don't become weary in well doing nor give up. Endure
hardship like a soldier, and don't get involve with
worldly things. Train your body to obey your spirit.

Daily Prayer

I thank You Heavenly Father for being with me today
and always. God, I ask that You protect me and my
family through the night and wake us up brand new
in the morning. In Jesus' name I pray, amen.

APRIL 24TH

TRANSFORMATIONAL MEDITATIONS

Daily Prayer

This is the day that the Lord has made, I will rejoice and be glad in it. In Jesus' name, amen.

"Scripture for the Day"
Exodus Chapters 13-16

PHRASE OF THE DAY

Love is everything, and without it, we are like tinkling brass. *"If I speak in the tongues of men and angels, but have not love, I am only a resounding gong or a clanging cymbal. If I have the gift of prophecy and can fathom all mysteries and all knowledge, and if I have faith that move mountains, but have not love, I am nothing. If I give away all I possess to the poor and surrender my body to the flames, but have not love, I gain nothing.*

1 Corinthians 13:1-3

APRIL 25TH

TRANSFORMATIONAL MEDITATIONS

"Scripture for the Day"
2nd Samuel Chapters 1-4

PHRASE OF THE DAY

You have been bought with a price and redeemed of all
your sins. You cannot be separated from the love of God.
You can do all things through Christ Jesus, amen.

Daily Prayer

As I close my eyes and lay my head down to sleep,
Lord cover me and give me sweet rest.

APRIL 26TH

TRANSFORMATIONAL MEDITATIONS

Daily Prayer

Father God, there is so much going on in the world right now, but Lord, I ask that You comfort my heart so that I will not be afraid. Give me peace so that I may be able to speak peace to others, especially to someone in need of a word from You.

"Scripture for the Day"
Psalm Chapters 48-50

PHRASE OF THE DAY

It is the parents' responsibility for the care and well-being of their family; the children are a direct reflection of their parents. Our Father God, has the same task to take care of His children. The question is, are you a child of God, and a reflection of Your Heavenly Father?

APRIL 27TH

TRANSFORMATIONAL MEDITATIONS

"Scripture for the Day"
Job Chapters 33-34

PHRASE OF THE DAY

Be still in the Lord and wait patiently for Him. Refrain from anger and turn from wrath which leads to evil.

Daily Prayer

Thank You Lord for being with me today. I know that You are with me always, and Lord, I thank You for every single moment, that You allow me to feel Your love and Your wonderful, peaceful and powerful presence.

APRIL 28TH

TRANSFORMATIONAL MEDITATIONS

Daily Prayer

Lord, help me to fall so deeply in love with You, that as I open my eyes each and every day, I will think of You first. Lead me and guide me today and help my mind to be alert and my soul to be consistently in perfect peace.

"Scripture for the Day"
Jeremiah Chapters 22-26

PHRASE OF THE DAY

We all need our lives covered by a person or a group of people with the authority to correct us. We need to be rebuked carefully, responsibly, and with love.

APRIL 29TH

TRANSFORMATIONAL MEDITATIONS

"Scripture for the Day"
Mark Chapters 13-14

PHRASE OF THE DAY

When we understand and rely on our own purpose, we run into difficulty. But it is God's purpose for your life that truly counts.

Daily Prayer

Lord, I know that tomorrow is not guaranteed, so right now I will give You all the thanks, and all the glory and all the praise before I lay my head down to sleep. I love You Lord and I thank You from the depths of my heart for all that You have done and are doing in my life as well as in the the lives of my family and my friends.

APRIL 30TH

TRANSFORMATIONAL MEDITATIONS

Daily Prayer

Heavenly Father, my Lord and my God, please
help me to spend more time with You today.

"Scripture for the Day"
2 Corinthians Chapters 4-5

PHRASE OF THE DAY

Today I speak death to that ungodly contract that you
have made that gave the gates of hell the right to judge
you; repent now. Now, I speak life and expansion of
your faith in your situation. Know without a shadow of
a doubt, that the Blood of Jesus Christ has been shed
for your Victory. If you agree say amen. Holy Spirit
flow and go to those who agree in Jesus' name.

MAY 1ST

TRANSFORMATIONAL MEDITATIONS

"Scripture for the Day"
Exodus Chapters 17-20

PHRASE OF THE DAY

Unfortunately, when God doesn't deliver when and how we think He should, we consult with which the Bible forbids, the world (familiar spirits) like Saul.

Daily Prayer

God, I thank You for being such a good God. You are truly amazing in every single way. Continue to lead and guide me my Lord, each and every day. In Jesus' name I pray, amen.

MAY 2ND

TRANSFORMATIONAL MEDITATIONS

Daily Prayer

Eyes have not seen and ears have not heard what the Lord has in store and has prepared for me. I thank You Lord Jesus, for having great things in store for me! Today will be a wonderful and glorious day, in Jesus' name I pray, amen.

"Scripture for the Day"
2nd Samuel Chapters 5-9

PHRASE OF THE DAY

Once you start renewing your mind with the Word of God, you must know that the familiar spirit (old man) is trying to get you back. If you go back, he will bring seven more with him and your new condition will be worse than your old. People dealing with addictions understand this, it's called a binge. I pray that this has taken off the blinders in Jesus' name.

MAY 3RD

TRANSFORMATIONAL MEDITATIONS

"Scripture for the Day"
Psalm Chapters 51-53

PHRASE OF THE DAY

When we don't understand someone or something, conflict
is unavoidable. Obtain understanding before saying
anything. Put on the word of peace on your feet and the
helmet of salvation. Don't be concerned and waste your time
with ungodly things that will just sidetrack your purpose.
Avoid arguing with a fool so as not to become one.

Daily Prayer

Lord, the world may reject and turn their backs on
me but thank You Lord for always loving me.

MAY 4TH

TRANSFORMATIONAL MEDITATIONS

Daily Prayer

Lord, it is in You that I live and that I breathe and that I have my being. Grant me the strength that I need this morning, Father God, to get through this entire day today. Thank You Lord, in Jesus' name for always hearing my prayers.

"Scripture for the Day"
Job Chapters 35-36

PHRASE OF THE DAY

No one can take away anything God has given us, but we can give it away. The enemy comes to steal, kill and destroy, so he is just doing his job, we can't blame him. If we do things to give our health and freedom away, then the enemy will take it. Read the Word and stop giving your life away; obedience is better than sacrifice.

MAY 5TH

TRANSFORMATIONAL MEDITATIONS

"Scripture for the Day"
Jeremiah Chapters 27-31

PHRASE OF THE DAY

Hey friends, God will not go against your will or what
you want in life. God does not make junk, so why do
we treat ourselves poorly? Please read God's will for
your life and put your will in sync, before you will
yourself to a place that was just made for the fallen.
I pray someone has ears to hear in Jesus' name.

Daily Prayer

Lord, help me to be more like You, each and every single
day. Protect me as I lay my head down to sleep this day
and wake me a new and refreshed in the morning.

MAY 6TH

TRANSFORMATIONAL MEDITATIONS

Daily Prayer

Lord, when people meet me and look at me God,
let my image be a mirrored reflection of You.

"Scripture for the Day"
Mark Chapters 15-16

PHRASE OF THE DAY

Whatever you're going through, God has His hand
on you. Stop feeding your fear and your fear will stop
growing. Trust in God and the smoke will clear quicker.

MAY 7TH

TRANSFORMATIONAL MEDITATIONS

"Scripture for the Day"
2nd Corinthians Chapters 6-8

PHRASE OF THE DAY

All authority in heaven and on earth has been given
to you through Jesus. Go make disciples of all,
baptizing in the name of the Father, Son, and
Holy Spirit.

Daily Prayer

Lord I thank You for this day. Today may not
have been perfect, but it was truly marvelous,
because You are always with me.

MAY 8TH

TRANSFORMATIONAL MEDITATIONS

Daily Prayer

O God, show me what my purpose is, and help me
not to get wrapped up in thinking of things that are
not lined up with Your perfect will for my life.

"Scripture for the Day"
Exodus Chapters 21-24

PHRASE OF THE DAY

To discipline means to instill moral and mental character,
you don't give values by punishing, you give values
by correcting. We all deeply desire discipline.

MAY 9TH

TRANSFORMATIONAL MEDITATIONS

"Scripture for the Day"
2nd Samuel Chapters 10-14

PHRASE OF THE DAY

We don't have to teach ourselves how to curse,
steal, lie, or be sexually immoral, for that is what
our flesh desires. We have to condition ourselves
with the Word to repel those behaviors. Amen.

Daily Prayer

The Lord is my light and my salvation; whom shall I fear?
The Lord is the strength of my life; of whom shall I be
afraid? Lord, help me not to fear and not to be afraid of
anything or anyone, no matter what the circumstance is.

MAY 10TH

TRANSFORMATIONAL MEDITATIONS

Daily Prayer

God, sometimes this life can get so lonely. Lord shower me with Your love and allow me to feel Your presence all day long, each and every single day.

"Scripture for the Day"
Psalm Chapters 54-56

PHRASE OF THE DAY

The tactic of the enemy is to keep us in our past. The Word says to forget those things from our past and press toward the future. If you were ever to drive a car forward while looking back, an accident would likely result. Whenever your past comes to your present it is trying to keep you from the future God has promised you. Give it to God and keep your eyes on Jesus. If you agree say amen.

MAY 11TH

TRANSFORMATIONAL MEDITATIONS

"Scripture for the Day"
Job Chapters 37-38

PHRASE OF THE DAY

Train up a child in the things of the Lord. You will be held accountable to God for what you do in front of His youth. Lead by example, for the youth does as they see.

Daily Prayer

I love You Lord, I ask that You please help me
to continuously desire to love You and to get
to know You more and more each day.

MAY 12TH

TRANSFORMATIONAL MEDITATIONS

Daily Prayer

Heavenly Father, I thank You for another day. Lord in the midst of hearing many different voices, Father God, help me to separate Your voice from the rest and to walk in obedience to what I trust and believe are Your clear instructions for my life.

"Scripture for the Day"
Jeremiah Chapters 32-36

PHRASE OF THE DAY

The believer's life is a fight against evil forces from without and temptation from within. If you stay true to God through it all, He promises you victory.

MAY 13TH

TRANSFORMATIONAL MEDITATIONS

"Scripture for the Day"
Luke Chapters 1-2

PHRASE OF THE DAY

Self-preservation is the way of the world; we have the toughest time understanding that. Peter denied Jesus three times because of self-preservation. The only good thing that comes out of this is our weakness. When we are weak the Holy Spirit shows up and gives us strength. Don't follow Jesus from a distance like Peter, but rather repent and come into His presence.

Daily Prayer

Father God, thank You for being with me, keeping me safe and protecting me throughout the day. Lord, teach me to trust Your Word to the point that when I hear it, I am able to say, *"Yes, Lord. It is and shall be so,"* and neither question it nor doubt it.

MAY 14TH

TRANSFORMATIONAL MEDITATIONS

Daily Prayer

Lord, teach me how to love and help me to always
have a cheerful, loving and giving heart. Show
me Lord, who I can help and care for today.

"Scripture for the Day"
2nd Corinthians Chapters 9-10

PHRASE OF THE DAY

Bitterness is one sin that will deplete your emotional
bank faster than any other. No matter what the cause it
will defile you. Forgive before your heart turns to stone,
and bitterness starts affecting every part of your life.

MAY 15TH

TRANSFORMATIONAL MEDITATIONS

"Scripture for the Day"
Exodus Chapters 25-28

PHRASE OF THE DAY

Father God, sometimes this cup feels like it is too much for me to bare, but I will persevere. I give myself to You, for I was bought at the ultimate price. My life is not my own, amen.

Daily Prayer

Lord, please give me more visions and more dreams and the ability to give interpretation to them. Make Your desires crystal clear to me so that I may put my hands to work for You, Your will and Your glory. Help me to follow every instruction and every detail to the fullest and to be neither worried nor concerned about my abilities. If You told me to do it, You will give me all that I need to accomplish the mission or the task. I decree this to be so in Jesus mighty and precious and wonderful name, Amen.

MAY 16ᵀᴴ

TRANSFORMATIONAL MEDITATIONS

Daily Prayer

Heavenly Father, please give me favor amongst the kings. Let my lifestyle and my walk in Your sight be worthy of favor. Let my light so shine in my obedience to You O God, that men will glorify You.

"Scripture for the Day"
2nd Samuel Chapters 15-19

PHRASE OF THE DAY

We are stuck sometimes because we get angry with the vessel God sent to unstick us with the truth and we won't receive the correction. God is not mocked.

MAY 17ᵀᴴ

TRANSFORMATIONAL MEDITATIONS

"Scripture for the Day"
Psalm Chapters 57-59

PHRASE OF THE DAY

Revelation knowledge is spiritual. Once you get experience of that, you understand that the gates of hell can't persuade you to do anything against who you are.

Daily Prayer

O God, I will run to You in the midst of my trials, my tests and all of my circumstances. I will trust in You O God, that You O God, will save me. For You are my deliverer, You are my Lord, my King and no one is greater than You. Let the traps that my enemies have set for me fall upon their own heads and those who mock me my Lord, bring them to shame. I will glorify You and praise Your holy name amongst all men, in Jesus' name I pray, amen. Amen. Amen.

MAY 18TH

TRANSFORMATIONAL MEDITATIONS

Daily Prayer

Lord, help me not to sin in my anger and help me not to let the sun go down on my anger as well. Give me a loving, caring and forgiving heart and help me to walk in Your perfect peace all the days of my life, inspite of my circumstances and all that goes on around me, in Jesus name, amen.

"Scripture for the Day"
Job Chapters 39-40

PHRASE OF THE DAY

Pride brings deception and reasoning with it. Feeling that God can use you to bless me but not correct me is wrongful thinking. Witchcraft and idolatry love pride.

MAY 19TH

TRANSFORMATIONAL MEDITATIONS

"Scripture for the Day"
Jeremiah Chapters 37-41

PHRASE OF THE DAY

A woman is a spiritual incubator who births spiritual results in God. She won't give up in prayer until she sees results. I thank God for all praying women, amen.

Daily Prayer

God, there most surely is no other God like You. You created the heavens; You created the earth, and You separated the seas. It was You alone and Your Holy Spirit and Wisdom who has created everything both in and above the seas. Lord, there most certainly is none like You. I praise You and I bless You my Lord. Goodnight. In Jesus' name, amen.

MAY 20TH

TRANSFORMATIONAL MEDITATIONS

Daily Prayer

O Lord, help me to pass my test the day my testing comes,
and help me O God, not to fear anything or anyone in both the
natural and in the spirit world and realm. In Jesus' name, amen.

"Scripture for the Day"
Luke Chapters 3-4

PHRASE OF THE DAY

Speak wisely making sure your information is
truthful and accurate, use your words to heal and fix
problems, not to blame. God is the ultimate judge.

MAY 21ST

TRANSFORMATIONAL MEDITATIONS

"Scripture for the Day"
2nd Corinthians Chapters 11-13

PHRASE OF THE DAY

Remain calm and gentle when confronting conflict,
and your example will become contagious. Add
value to everyone that contacts you, even when you
disagree. Be quick to apologize when wrong. I pray
these words touch your core, in Jesus' name.

Daily Prayer

Lord, increase my discernment that I may never be tricked
or deceived by the false prophets on this earth. Let my light
so shine that no darkness may penetrate or overtake me.

MAY 22ND

TRANSFORMATIONAL MEDITATIONS

Daily Prayer

Heavenly Father, show me the gifts that You have given me. Help me to creatively use my gifts for Your Kingdom's purposes and for Your name sake. In Jesus' name, amen.

"Scripture for the Day"
Exodus Chapters 29-32

PHRASE OF THE DAY

Every tongue that rises against us, God will condemn, especially our own tongue. We normally are the first tongue that rises toward ourselves. We are the head and not the tail, above and not beneath. We are a chosen people.

MAY 23RD

TRANSFORMATIONAL MEDITATIONS

"Scripture for the Day"
2nd Samuel Chapters 20-24

PHRASE OF THE DAY

How you are living, free or in captivity, is a direct
result of how you are thinking. If you're not renewing
your mind with the Word, freedom is unattainable.

Daily Prayer

Lord, let me walk amongst men as a drop of water to
the deserts sand leading them to the river of running
water, O God, so that they may thirst no more.

MAY 24TH

TRANSFORMATIONAL MEDITATIONS

Daily Prayer

Heavenly Father and my God, without You I am nothing. Lord keep my heart humble and in sync with Your heart Lord Jesus. Let me not go astray and worship anyone or anything, but You.

"Scripture for the Day"
Psalm Chapters 60-62

PHRASE OF THE DAY

We need to know the weapons of the enemy, so that we will not be deceived by fear, loneliness, fornication, drugs, and the like. God's way is a repellent for those weapons.

MAY 25TH

TRANSFORMATIONAL MEDITATIONS

"Scripture for the Day"
Job Chapters 41-42

PHRASE OF THE DAY

Yesterday in my time with the Lord, He revealed to me that a storm was coming laced with depression and low self-esteem; gear up! I told the Lord in prayer that we really don't need anything else to plague the body of Christ. So, agree with me, what is bound in heaven is also bound on earth. We take authority and send that storm back to the pit, in Jesus' name.

Daily Prayer

Lord, make my latter days, greater than the rest.

MAY 26TH

TRANSFORMATIONAL MEDITATIONS

Daily Prayer

Heavenly Father, thank you once again for waking me up this morning. Lord, all that I ask of You today, is that You please order my steps in Your will. Tell me where to go and when. Show me what to do and how to do it. Lead and guide me O Lord, that I may not sin against You or turn the wrong way. Protect me Father and keep me safe from all hurt, harm and danger. Protect me from the evil one this day, both now and forever more. In Jesus' name I pray, amen.

"Scripture for the Day"
Jeremiah Chapters 42-46

PHRASE OF THE DAY

The body of Christ is suffering from identity crisis. If we don't know who and what we are, when the trial shows up, we will fold. The battle is not yours but God's.

MAY 27TH

TRANSFORMATIONAL MEDITATIONS

"Scripture for the Day"
Luke Chapters 5-6

PHRASE OF THE DAY

When Jesus called Lazarus from the grave, He told them to take off his grave clothes. To us the grave clothes represents the old mindset. So, Jesus is saying, come out and change your mindset of drunkenness, sexual immortality, lying, doubt, stealing, hatred, idolatry, sicknesses and any other wrongdoing.

Daily Prayer

O God, how I have toiled and toiled and toiled. Show me when and where I may cast my net, that my work may not be in vain.

MAY 28TH

TRANSFORMATIONAL MEDITATIONS

Daily Prayer

Heavenly Father and my God, help me Lord, to desire only to please You. Help me Lord, to not compromise my faith and my beliefs in order to gain man's approval. Help me God to not want to please man, but to please You and to put You first above all. Lord Jesus, help me to always put You first.

"Scripture for the Day"
Galatians Chapters 1-3

PHRASE OF THE DAY

Thank You Father God, that we have redemption through the blood of Jesus and the forgiveness of our trespasses, according to the riches of His grace. Ephesians 1:7

MAY 29TH

TRANSFORMATIONAL MEDITATIONS

"Scripture for the Day"
Exodus Chapters 33-36

PHRASE OF THE DAY

Broken relationships can hinder our relationship with God. If we have a grievance with a friend, we should fix it quickly. Loving God and hating man equals deception.

Daily Prayer

Lord, teach me how to saturate in Your presence O Lord. Help me to abide in You as You abide in me.

MAY 30TH

TRANSFORMATIONAL MEDITATIONS

Daily Prayer

Heavenly Father, grant me favor O Lord. Give me
more wisdom and increase my discernment, so
that I may know what is and is not of You.

"Scripture for the Day"
1st Kings Chapters 1-4

PHRASE OF THE DAY

If anyone is prodigal right now, there is no place
like our Father's house. Make the right choice now
and repent and follow Jesus back to the Father.

MAY 31ST

TRANSFORMATIONAL MEDITATIONS

"Scripture for the Day"
Psalm Chapters 63-65

PHRASE OF THE DAY

Lord, help me to be strong and courageous as it says in
Your Word we ought to be. Help me Heavenly Father,
to not be afraid or terrified because of my enemies, for
You Lord go with me everywhere that I go. I stand on
Your Word Lord, trusting and believing that You will
never leave me nor forsake me. Deuteronomy 31:6

Daily Prayer

O God, silence the lips of my enemies and those
who lie against me. For You O Lord, are my God.
Help me Lord to do better and to be better in all
things concerning You, in every area of my life.

JUNE 1ST

TRANSFORMATIONAL MEDITATIONS

Daily Prayer

Lord, help me to know wisdom and to perceive the
words of understanding. Help me Lord to continuously
walk in obedience to Your instructions and
Your word.

"Scripture for the Day"
Proverbs Chapter 1

PHRASE OF THE DAY

It takes intense heat to purify gold. That same heat is
required in trials for the believer to be purified. Trials show
what's in us, when exposed, it's our job to deal with it.

JUNE 2ND

TRANSFORMATIONAL MEDITATIONS

"Scripture for the Day"
Jeremiah Chapters 47-52

PHRASE OF THE DAY

Hardening is like a callus or like tough bone fibers that bind a fracture. Spiritual hardening begins with self-sufficiency, security in oneself, and self-satisfaction. The real danger is that at some point, repeated resistance to God will yield an actual inability to respond, which the Bible describes as hardening of heart. Insensitivity indicates advanced hardening.

Daily Prayer

Father God, in the mighty name of Jesus, I repent this day, for all of my sins, both those committed knowingly and unknowingly. Spare me Lord and be a shield around me in Your time of wrath, that I may not be destroyed and counted as being among the wicked. Guard my mouth and order my steps in Your will.

JUNE 3RD

TRANSFORMATIONAL MEDITATIONS

Daily Prayer

God, give me a humble heart and help me
to submit all my ways to You.

"Scripture for the Day"
Luke Chapters 7-8

PHRASE OF THE DAY

The tongue that brings healing is a tree of life,
but a deceitful tongue crushes the spirit.

JUNE 4TH

TRANSFORMATIONAL MEDITATIONS

"Scripture for the Day"
Galatians Chapters 4-6

PHRASE OF THE DAY

It is hard to argue with someone who insists on speaking gently. Turn away wrath and seek peace using gentle words. Try it, you might enjoy it, plus it's the Word of God.

Daily Prayer

Lord, tonight, I cast my cares to You. Help me not to pick them up again Lord, but to hand them over completely to You. It is neither Your will nor Your desire to have us all stressed out. I surrender all to You. Help me to walk in love and to walk in peace, all the days of my life, in Jesus' name, amen.

JUNE 5TH

TRANSFORMATIONAL MEDITATIONS

Daily Prayer

Lord, Your wisdom is like no other. There is truly
none like You. Today, I just want to adore You
and give You praise. I serve an incredible and a
magnificent God. I am in aww of Your wonders.

"Scripture for the Day"
Exodus Chapters 37-40

PHRASE OF THE DAY

Lord, as it says in Joshua 1:9, help me to be strong and
courageous and not afraid. Help me Lord, to not be
discouraged, for You Lord will be with me wherever I go.

JUNE 6TH

TRANSFORMATIONAL MEDITATIONS

"Scripture for the Day"
1st Kings Chapters 5-9

PHRASE OF THE DAY

Thank the Lord this day for His unfailing love and put your trust in Him. Ask Him to show you which way you should go and put your life in His hands surrendering all to Him.

Daily Prayer

Lord, let Your desires be my desires and my desires line up with Your Word. I offer to You, as You sit on Your throne, a special offering of thanksgiving and of praise. For You alone are worthy God, and to You alone I will give praise.

JUNE 7TH

TRANSFORMATIONAL MEDITATIONS

Daily Prayer

O Lord, there is none like You. This morning my
Lord, I just want to adore You. I just want to give Your
mighty and wonderful name all of the honor and all of
the praise. How magnificent You are, O mighty God.
This morning I will give You praise. I love You Father,
and I glorify Your all powerful and mighty name.

"Scripture for the Day"
Psalm Chapters 66-68

PHRASE OF THE DAY

A backslider is filled with his own ways, and the
Lord's ways are out of his reach. They are usually
angry and unhappy with themselves and God's people.
I pray that they will return to God's grace so that
their steps may be guided down the right path.

JUNE 8TH

TRANSFORMATIONAL MEDITATIONS

"Scripture for the Day"
Proverbs Chapters 2-3

PHRASE OF THE DAY

If we are believers, we will suffer persecution; the Word says so. If you die to self, it won't hurt as much. Help someone else, and you will go through quicker.

Daily Prayer

Lord, I accept Your words and do not argue with them. Help me Father God to continuously store them up within me, through reading the scriptures, through writing, through studying and through fasting and praying. I seek to understand You and Your Word more and more. Father God, grant me more wisdom and favor that I may set a great example of what it means to be a follower of Jesus Christ. Halleluiah, and amen, amen and amen.

JUNE 9TH

TRANSFORMATIONAL MEDITATIONS

Daily Prayer

Heavenly Father, this morning I ask my Lord, that You will have mercy on all of Your people. Forgive those who have backslidden and have fallen into the traps of the enemy. Do not forget Your people Lord. Send a messenger, send an angel, send Your people a way out of bondage and out of captivity. Give them a heart that will repent and turn back to You. Embrace them with Your love and Your kindness and forgive them O Lord. Forgive them for their faults, their mistakes and all of their sins. Repent all yee nations so that the Lord God almighty may rain down justice and heal your land and forgive your sins and heal the wounds of the broken hearted.

"Scripture for the Day"
The Book of Lamentations

PHRASE OF THE DAY

Unbelievers are not only those who have not come to Christ, but they are also those, due to their unbelief, who cannot enter the supernatural dimensions of the Kingdom of God.

JUNE 10TH

TRANSFORMATIONAL MEDITATIONS

"Scripture for the Day"
Luke Chapters 9-10

PHRASE OF THE DAY

Where the Spirit of the Lord is, there is liberty. You should have freedom to let the Holy Spirit flow wherever you go, bringing salvation, healing, and deliverance.

Daily Prayer

God, I am smiling tonight, because of how magnificent and wonderful You are. You truly are a God of miracles and I have nothing to fear. It was You, O Lord, that took the 5 loaves and the 2 fish and multiplied them and fed the thousands. It was You who healed the eyes of the blind, made the deaf to hear and the lame to walk. O God perform Your miracles through me. Perform Your miracles in not only my life but in the lives of all those who I love and care deeply for that are around me and in my family. I thank You, Lord God, for being such an amazing and all-powerful God and I thank You Lord Jesus for always hearing me. In Jesus' name I pray, amen, amen and amen!

JUNE 11TH

TRANSFORMATIONAL MEDITATIONS

Daily Prayer

Heavenly Father, my God, my King, I want to thank and give You glory and praise for calling and choosing me. Thank You, Lord, for setting me aside and for knowing me from the inside out, even better than I or anyone else ever could. I thank You Lord God that I am special in Your sight, and precious in Your eyes. Lord today, I embrace my differences and embrace the God in me. Help me to continuously grow and get better each and every day. I want You to be proud of me. I want to bring You joy. I love You God, but I want to love You even more, in Jesus' name, amen.

"Scripture for the Day"
Ephesians Chapters 1-3

PHRASE OF THE DAY

Contrary to what the world might say God loves you. He sent His only Son to prove it. The way of the world is what slowly separates us from God and not His LOVE.

JUNE 12TH

TRANSFORMATIONAL MEDITATIONS

"Scripture for the Day"
Leviticus Chapters 1-3

PHRASE OF THE DAY

God will extend His grace to those
who are humble before Him.

Daily Prayer

Have Your way with me my Lord. Have Your way in my
life. Help me to completely surrender to You daily, every
morning, every evening and every night. Let me speak
the way You want me to speak, in a way that is pleasant
and pleasing to You. Lord, I pray that I will have the
mindset of Christ Jesus and surrender all my thoughts to
You. I give them all to You Lord and lay them this day
at Your feet. Thank You, Jesus, thank You Lord. I ask
these things in Jesus' name, amen, amen and amen.

JUNE 13TH

TRANSFORMATIONAL MEDITATIONS

Daily Prayer

O God, I pray that my heart will never turn away from You. I reverence You my Lord and my God. Help me to keep You as number one in both my heart and mind and to carry You around in my spirit always, all the day long. Remove any idols from my life that I may not even know are there. Forgive me Lord if I have indeed already committed any great sin against You. Put me and keep me on track to serve no other god, but You, the one and true living God; for there is none like You.

"Scripture for the Day"
1st Kings Chapters 10-13

PHRASE OF THE DAY

God is looking in this season for believers like Joseph and Daniel, who will not compromise no matter what the trial. We need to start living like we're dying.

JUNE 14TH

TRANSFORMATIONAL MEDITATIONS

"Scripture for the Day"
Psalm Chapters 69-71

PHRASE OF THE DAY

A believer will backslide when they do not function in
their gifting or calling. They will then also begin to use
God's gift for their own benefit, not to protect and serve.

Daily Prayer

O God, help me not to ever be consumed or overwhelmed
by any circumstances that life may bring. I know that You
know and remember that we are merely humans that were
formed by Your hands from the dust. But God, with Your help,
strength, loving kindness and everlasting power, we can do
such great and wonderful things. Touch my heart Lord and
give me peace to know that no matter what may be going on
in my life and the lives of my family and loved ones, it is well,
and You even now, are holding me in the palm of Your hands.
I thank You God for Your divine protection and Your love.
Goodnight my God. Please protect me and keep my family
and I safe as we sleep. Give us sweet rest and a knowing deep
down in our hearts that it is well. In Jesus' name, it is well.

JUNE 15TH

TRANSFORMATIONAL MEDITATIONS

Daily Prayer

Lord, let me not turn away from wisdom, but rather, embrace it, welcoming it into my daily life, mind and heart. Help me to practice all that I have learned from You as I read Your Word and as I get direction from those who were placed as leaders and teachers over me.

"Scripture for the Day"
Proverbs Chapter 4

PHRASE OF THE DAY

Sin deceives people by misusing the law. Satan took Eve's mind off the freedom she had and put it on the restriction God made. Keeping the law doesn't save us.

JUNE 16TH

TRANSFORMATIONAL MEDITATIONS

"Scripture for the Day"
Ezekiel Chapters 1-6

PHRASE OF THE DAY

God permits storms in our lives to expose weakness. We
are only as strong as the storms we survive. You have
not seen nor heard, what God is about to do for you.

Daily Prayer

Lord, my Lord, help me not to run away from my calling.
If I am called to be a teacher Lord, help me to teach. If I
am called to be a preacher Lord, help me to be fearless
and speak. If I am called to be a prophet Lord, allow
me to boldly speak Your Word. Whatever I am called
to be Lord, help me to know and to trust that You are
and forever will always be right there with me.

JUNE 17TH

TRANSFORMATIONAL MEDITATIONS

Daily Prayer

Heavenly Father, teach me how to pray. Teach me how to knock, so that doors may be opened. Teach me how to persistently seek after You, so that all that I seek I may find in You. Teach me how to have a deeper relationship with You Lord, so that I may learn how to come boldly to Your throne with the utmost confidence, knowing that You are always there and that You always hear me. I ask You Father God for help and for anything that I may stand in need of. You are my Heavenly Father, and I am Your child and I, by the blood of Jesus, have the right to ask, seek and knock; knowing that You will answer each and every single prayer Your way and in Your time, amen.

"Scripture for the Day"
Luke Chapters 11-12

PHRASE OF THE DAY

Lord, Your Word says that if anyone is in Christ, they are a new creation and the old has gone, and the new is here! Help me God to walk in the newness of my new Life in Christ Jesus, amen.

JUNE 18TH

TRANSFORMATIONAL MEDITATIONS

"Scripture for the Day"
Ephesians Chapters 4-6

PHRASE OF THE DAY

The Lord goes before you. He is always with you. He
will never fail to protect you. Therefore, you should
not fear anyone or anything, nor be anxious.

Daily Prayer

Lord, help me to live a life daily that is pleasing to You.
Help me to walk, talk and live according to the calling
that You have purposed and ordained for my life. Lord,
please make my paths plain and clear and easy for me to
see. I want to live at a higher standard and bring glory and
honor to Your majestic, wonderful and glorious name.

JUNE 19TH

TRANSFORMATIONAL MEDITATIONS

Daily Prayer

Help me Father to be aware of Your presence every single
day. If I sin or fall short Lord, help me to repent and ask for
forgiveness immediately. Let me never be comfortable in any
kind of wrongdoing, but to be God conscious continually.

"Scripture for the Day"
Leviticus Chapters 4-6

PHRASE OF THE DAY

Lord, help us to be on our guard and to stand firm
in the faith, being courageous and strong.

JUNE 20TH

TRANSFORMATIONAL MEDITATIONS

"Scripture for the Day"
1st Kings Chapters 14-18

PHRASE OF THE DAY

Talking about things that irritate you keeps the
fire of anger going. Learning to get passed them
cuts the fuel line and makes the fire die out.

Daily Prayer

Lord, let me cause no man or woman to sin. Deliver
me O God from all evil and help me to walk in my
deliverance so that You can use me to set others free.

JUNE 21ST

TRANSFORMATIONAL MEDITATIONS

Daily Prayer

Heavenly Father, You are my strength. I am nothing without You. I dedicate my life to You a fresh and a new this day O Lord. Please forgive me for all of my sins and help me to forgive myself, and anyone who has hurt me, or wounded my heart. As You set me free and deliver me, help me Lord to set them free from my heart so that I may walk in love and not in anger. I will offer up a sacrifice of praise. I love You my Lord and I thank You for Your goodness, Your kindness, Your faithfulness and Your love. In Jesus' name I pray, amen.

"Scripture for the Day"
Psalm Chapters 72-74

PHRASE OF THE DAY

Lord, I come to You this day with all of my burdens and weariness, please give me rest.

JUNE 22ND

TRANSFORMATIONAL MEDITATIONS

"Scripture for the Day"
Proverbs Chapters 5-6

PHRASE OF THE DAY

Love is not an option; it is the highest and holy commandment that Jesus gave to us. The blood and all what we believe originated from love. God is love.

Daily Prayer

Lord, help me to not worry or even be the slightest bit concerned about my life or my enemies, for I know that the very same traps that they set for my feet, they will fall in. You are my Lord, my Savior, My God and my King, I have nothing to fear. I will not be stressed out and worried. I will not be afraid. I seal this prayer with the Blood of Jesus Christ and it is in Jesus' name that I pray, amen, amen and amen.

JUNE 23RD

TRANSFORMATIONAL MEDITATIONS

Daily Prayer

Lord, help me not to become like the hypocrites that You speak of in Your Word. Let me not have 2 faces, being holy in the day and in the night entertaining the dark world. Help me to live the same way in both my personal and private life, as well as before the world in the public and in the open each and every day. You are a God that can see in both day and night. Nothing is hidden from You.

"Scripture for the Day"
Ezekiel Chapters 7-12

PHRASE OF THE DAY

The Spirit God gave us does not make us timid, but gives us power, love and self-discipline. Walk in the Spirit so that you do not fulfill the lusts of the flesh.

JUNE 24TH

TRANSFORMATIONAL MEDITATIONS

"Scripture for the Day"
Luke Chapters 13-14

PHRASE OF THE DAY

A true shepherd will grow and mature sheep, but a hireling (someone who works only for pay) will tarnish the sheep turning them into goats, spiritually. Goats buck.

Daily Prayer

O Lord, please don't cut me down. Prune me so that I may become healthier and stronger and bear much fruit in Your sight. Let me not grow bad fruit or no fruit at all. I want to make You so proud of me. I want to be pleasing in Your eyes. I love You Jesus; I give You permission to prune me and to till the soil around me that I may bear good fruit.

JUNE 25TH

TRANSFORMATIONAL MEDITATIONS

Daily Prayer

Lord, help me not to pray just for myself, but to also pray for all those around me and for our Nation.

"Scripture for the Day"
Philippians Chapters 1-2

PHRASE OF THE DAY

Jesus assures us that unless a man is born again (anew, from above), he cannot ever see (know, be acquainted with, and experience) the Kingdom of God.

JUNE 26TH

TRANSFORMATIONAL MEDITATIONS

"Scripture for the Day"
Leviticus Chapters 7-9

PHRASE OF THE DAY

The joy of the Lord is your strength. Rejoice and give God thanks and give God praises today, no matter what the situation looks like. God is able and is still seated on the throne. All things are possible with Him.

Daily Prayer

Lord, tonight I just want to say thank You Lord. Thank You for being a sacrifice for me. It is because of You that my sins are forgiven and I may have eternal life. Lord Jesus, all the good that I have is all because of You. You died on a cross at Calvary for me and because of that, I am able to be set free. Your Word says that if I confess with my mouth and believe in my heart that Jesus Christ is Lord and the only begotten Son of God, who died and was risen from the grave and now sits at the right hand of God, I shall be saved. Lord I confess right now that because of You Lord Jesus, I have been set free! You alone are God and I ask You Lord Jesus to come into my heart and be Lord and ruler over my life so that I may be saved. In Jesus' name I pray, amen, amen and amen.

JUNE 27ᵀᴴ

TRANSFORMATIONAL MEDITATIONS

Daily Prayer

Lord, I ask You this morning, God, I ask You today, please remove anyone from my life that is not any good for me. Remove all those people who should not be around me. But don't leave me alone Father God. Send into my life people that I can learn from. People that will lovingly and willingly help me in my relationship and my walk with You. Send into my life, Believers that truly love You Lord Jesus and that whole heartedly serve You and let me also be a blessing to them, in Jesus' name, amen.

"Scripture for the Day"
1st Kings Chapters 19-22

PHRASE OF THE DAY

When your ways meet up with God's way, you can either change your way by not leaning on your understanding or stay in bondage to sin and death.

JUNE 28TH

TRANSFORMATIONAL MEDITATIONS

"Scripture for the Day"
Psalm Chapters 75-77

PHRASE OF THE DAY

Being carnal is not just a problem for unbelievers, but it's a mindset we have to change by renewing our minds.

Daily Prayer

Thank You Father God, for protecting and keeping me safe from all danger today O Lord. Life may not always go the way that we would like it to. Sometimes we make mistakes, things happen; life happens. Although my life may not seem perfect right now, as I have my share of problems, I am able to endure the ups and downs, because of You Father. I am thankful though, in the midst of all of my situations that I have You. Thank You for always being there for me. God, I need You and am thankful for You.

JUNE 29TH

TRANSFORMATIONAL MEDITATIONS

Daily Prayer

Lord help me to meditate on Your Word throughout the day, so that I may grow not only stronger and stronger, but that I may grow closer to You. I want to be more like You Jesus. Touch my heart, my mind and my spirit and soul today. Give me a clean heart Lord and renew in me a right spirit, that I may not sin against You. Forgive me for all of my past sins. Today is a new day. Help me to be better, wiser and full of more courage today and to let all that is in the past go and to leave it all behind me.

"Scripture for the Day"
Proverbs Chapter 7

PHRASE OF THE DAY

Lord, prepare my heart, my mind and my spirit, so that I may bodly say with all that is within me, *"Hear I am Lord, send me."*

JUNE 30TH

TRANSFORMATIONAL MEDITATIONS

"Scripture for the Day"
Ezekiel Chapters 13-18

PHRASE OF THE DAY

Lord, You are faithful, strengthen and protect
Your people from the evil one.

Daily Prayer

God, there is truly none like You. I adore You Father and
am forever grateful to have You in my life. If it wasn't for
You my Lord, I would not be here. I owe it all to You. It's
You that has kept me safe Lord. It is You that has been right
there by myside. Thank You Father for Your love, Your
gentleness, Your correction, Your goodness, Your mercy and
Your kindness. Thank You also for being so patient with me.
Help me Father to apply all that I have learned these past
several months and I pray that my living be not in vein.

Closing Prayer

Lord, thank You for Your divine protection and love and for keeping me safe throughout the 1st half of the year. As I step into the 2nd half of this year, continue to lead and guide me Lord. I pray that it will be even better and greater than the days behind me. By faith I am looking forward to the rest of the year in hope for better and more glorious days. Thank You Lord, for all that You do and for all that You have done in my life and in the lives of my loved ones. Bless our later days O God, let them be greater than the rest. I ask this in Jesus' mighty, glorious and precious name, amen. You are wonderful Lord. Bless Your Holy name.

TRANSFORMATIONAL MEDITATIONS

2ND HALF OF THE YEAR

Opening Prayer

Lord, as I enter into the 2nd half of this year, help me to
pray my Daily Prayers boldly, sincerely and humbly to You
comfortably from my heart and from within. I now know
and understand that prayer is just talking to You O God
and that there are no right or wrong ways to pray as long as
I am honest in my expressions towards You. I now know
and understand that I may speak freely and that I just need
to be me! Thank you, God, for teaching me how to pray
and how to be free, to be me, in You! I love You Lord, help
me to be honest and to be a positive reflection of You.

JULY 1ST

TRANSFORMATIONAL MEDITATIONS

"Scripture for the Day"
Luke Chapters 15-16

PHRASE OF THE DAY

Without understanding, life is an experiment, and frustration
is the reward. When problems come, and we don't understand
the problems, much less life, we fake it. I believe there is
a lot of faking going on in some churches today due to the
lack of understanding. Let's meditate on God's Word and
pray for wisdom that will lead us to truth and salvation.

Daily Prayer

_____

_____

_____

_____

_____

JULY 2ND

TRANSFORMATIONAL MEDITATIONS

Daily Prayer

_____

_____

_____

_____

_____

"Scripture for the Day"
Philippians Chapters 3-4

_____

PHRASE OF THE DAY

Let all bitterness, wrath, anger, and evil speaking be put
away from you with all malice. Be kind to each other,
compassionate and forgiving as God has forgiven you.

JULY 3RD

TRANSFORMATIONAL MEDITATIONS

"Scripture for the Day"
Leviticus Chapters 10-12

PHRASE OF THE DAY

Out of faith, hope, and love; the greatest of the three is love. Love is and action word. How can you love God who you have not seen, and not love His people?

Daily Prayer

_____

_____

_____

_____

_____

JULY 4TH

TRANSFORMATIONAL MEDITATIONS

Daily Prayer

_____

_____

_____

_____

_____

"Scripture for the Day"
2nd Kings Chapters 1-5

PHRASE OF THE DAY

When an evil spirit comes out of a man, it goes through dry places seeking rest and finds none. Then it says, I will return to the house where I left. When it arrives and finds it unoccupied, it returns and brings seven others. Just cleaning up one's life without filling it with God is a dangerous task, for the demons will come back with their friends. My people are destroyed for lack of knowledge. Let's pray for wisdom. Amen.

JULY 5TH

TRANSFORMATIONAL MEDITATIONS

"Scripture for the Day"
Psalm Chapters 78-80

PHRASE OF THE DAY

We must never forget that God is our refuge and strength,
an ever-present help in trouble. Run to Him and He
will guide you and be your help and strength.

Daily Prayer

JULY 6TH

TRANSFORMATIONAL MEDITATIONS

Daily Prayer

_____

_____

_____

_____

_____

"Scripture for the Day"
Proverbs Chapters 8-9

PHRASE OF THE DAY

Everything that God allows us to go through in our life is
indeed for a reason, even though it doesn't look like it at times.
Whatever has happened in your life be comforted in knowing
that God will work all things for the good of those who love
Him and who have been called according to His purpose.

JULY 7TH

TRANSFORMATIONAL MEDITATIONS

"Scripture for the Day"
Ezekiel Chapters 19-24

PHRASE OF THE DAY

Do you know that you are God's handiwork,
created in Christ Jesus to do good works,
which God prepared in advance for us?

Daily Prayer

_____

_____

_____

_____

_____

JULY 8TH

TRANSFORMATIONAL MEDITATIONS

Daily Prayer

_____

_____

_____

_____

_____

"Scripture for the Day"
Luke Chapters 17-18

PHRASE OF THE DAY

There is always a distance between the promise and
the possession and that distance is NEVER uneventful,
but is designed to build your faith in God.

JULY 9TH

TRANSFORMATIONAL MEDITATIONS

"Scripture for the Day"
Colossians Chapters 1-2

PHRASE OF THE DAY

To discourage is to deprive of courage, hope, or
confidence, dishearten, or dispirit. To Encourage is
to inspire with courage, spirit, or confidence.
Choose one please.

Daily Prayer

_____

_____

_____

_____

_____

JULY 10TH

TRANSFORMATIONAL MEDITATIONS

Daily Prayer

_____

_____

_____

_____

_____

"Scripture for the Day"
Leviticus Chapters 13-15

PHRASE OF THE DAY

Emotions are feelings of happiness, sorrow, fear, or hate.
Your emotions have been trained on what to do while
you were growing up, but for most of us, we were trained
in the wrong way. Your emotions should be an asset to
you not a debt. Retrain, using the Word, and nothing
will be able to stop God's purpose for your life.

JULY 11TH

TRANSFORMATIONAL MEDITATIONS

"Scripture for the Day"
2nd Kings Chapters 6-10

PHRASE OF THE DAY

Don't be discouraged, Satan may blow and yell, but there is nothing he can do to stop you; providing you continue to trust in the Lord.

Daily Prayer

_____

_____

_____

_____

_____

JULY 12TH

TRANSFORMATIONAL MEDITATIONS

Daily Prayer

_____

_____

_____

_____

_____

"Scripture for the Day"
Psalm Chapters 81-83

PHRASE OF THE DAY

Wherever you find faith you will see God's presence. God
doesn't dwell where there is disbelief. We walk by faith not
by sight. Seek His face daily and watch what He can do.

JULY 13TH

TRANSFORMATIONAL MEDITATIONS

"Scripture for the Day"
Proverbs Chapter 10

PHRASE OF THE DAY

If your enemy is hungry, feed him, if he is
thirsty, give him a drink. Do not be overcome
by evil, but overcome evil with good.

Daily Prayer

_____

_____

_____

_____

_____

JULY 14TH

TRANSFORMATIONAL MEDITATIONS

Daily Prayer

_____

_____

_____

_____

_____

"Scripture for the Day"
Ezekiel Chapters 25-30

PHRASE OF THE DAY

In this world we will have trouble, but take heart!
Jesus has overcome the world.

JULY 15TH

TRANSFORMATIONAL MEDITATIONS

"Scripture for the Day"
Luke Chapters 19-20

PHRASE OF THE DAY

Seek first the kingdom of God and all His righteousness
and all these things will be given to you.

Daily Prayer

_____

_____

_____

_____

_____

JULY 16TH

TRANSFORMATIONAL MEDITATIONS

Daily Prayer

_____

_____

_____

_____

_____

"Scripture for the Day"
Colossians Chapters 3-4

PHRASE OF THE DAY

I remember impatiently wanting the power that God says I
should have without the fruit being developed. Love, joy,
peace, longsuffering, gentleness, goodness, faith, meekness,
and self-control. Allow the fruit to develop.
Study the Word of God.

JULY 17TH

TRANSFORMATIONAL MEDITATIONS

"Scripture for the Day"
Leviticus Chapters 16-18

PHRASE OF THE DAY

The peace of God, which transcends all understanding,
will guard your heart and your mind in Christ Jesus.
Receive it in Jesus name today and everyday.

Daily Prayer

_____

_____

_____

_____

_____

JULY 18TH

TRANSFORMATIONAL MEDITATIONS

Daily Prayer

_____

_____

_____

_____

_____

"Scripture for the Day"
2nd Kings Chapters 11-15

PHRASE OF THE DAY

A lot of believers still think the way the world thinks and
instead of going to the Word, they go to worldly things. Be
transformed by renewing your mind with God's words.

JULY 19TH

TRANSFORMATIONAL MEDITATIONS

"Scripture for the Day"
Psalm Chapters 84-86

PHRASE OF THE DAY

Submit yourself to God and resist the devil so
he may flee. Whatever you feed will grow.

Daily Prayer

_____

_____

_____

_____

_____

JULY 20TH

TRANSFORMATIONAL MEDITATIONS

Daily Prayer

_____

_____

_____

_____

_____

"Scripture for the Day"
Proverbs Chapters 11-12

PHRASE OF THE DAY

When a believer finds themselves under a true apostolic
mantel, they will begin to move towards their calling
and will see themselves in a different way.

JULY 21ST

TRANSFORMATIONAL MEDITATIONS

"Scripture for the Day"
Ezekiel Chapters 31-36

PHRASE OF THE DAY

The Word of God is healing to your body, food for
your soul, light in darkness, faith over fear, way where
there is no way, and life instead of death; pass it on.

Daily Prayer

_____

_____

_____

_____

_____

JULY 22ND

TRANSFORMATIONAL MEDITATIONS

Daily Prayer

_____

_____

_____

_____

_____

"Scripture for the Day"
Luke Chapters 21-22

PHRASE OF THE DAY

Whoever finds me, finds life and obtains favor from the Lord, but they who sin against me wrongs his own soul. Who am I?

TRANSFORMATIONAL MEDITATIONS

"Scripture for the Day"
1st Thessalonians Chapters 1-3

PHRASE OF THE DAY

The more we know about the spiritual world, the easier it will be to apply the principles of light, which will drive out darkness, for a victorious church.

Daily Prayer

_____

_____

_____

_____

_____

JULY 24TH

TRANSFORMATIONAL MEDITATIONS

Daily Prayer

_____

_____

_____

_____

_____

"Scripture for the Day"
Leviticus Chapters 19-21

PHRASE OF THE DAY

Let all bitterness, wrath, anger, and evil speaking be put
away from you with all malice. Be kind to each other,
compassionate and forgiving as God has forgiven you.

JULY 25TH

TRANSFORMATIONAL MEDITATIONS

"Scripture for the Day"
2nd Kings Chapters 16-20

PHRASE OF THE DAY

The Lord has declared in His Word that He knows the plans
that He has for you, plans to prosper you and not to harm
you, plans to give you hope and a future. Will you believe?

Daily Prayer

_____

_____

_____

_____

_____

JULY 26TH

TRANSFORMATIONAL MEDITATIONS

Daily Prayer

_____

_____

_____

_____

_____

"Scripture for the Day"
Psalm Chapters 87-89

PHRASE OF THE DAY

There are three roadblocks in life: they know nothing,
they understand nothing, they walk about in darkness
and all the foundations of the earth are shaken.
Psalm 82: 5. Look at the morals of our nation.

JULY 27TH

TRANSFORMATIONAL MEDITATIONS

"Scripture for the Day"
Proverbs Chapter 13

PHRASE OF THE DAY

Question saints, if you were in prison with bail and I
paid it on the 1st of July but for whatever the reason
you got out today, what day was your freedom?

Daily Prayer

_____

_____

_____

_____

_____

JULY 28TH

TRANSFORMATIONAL MEDITATIONS

Daily Prayer

_____

_____

_____

_____

_____

"Scripture for the Day"
Ezekiel Chapters 37-42

PHRASE OF THE DAY

Be strong and of a good courage, God is with you.
So fear not and do not be afraid of your enemies, for
God will not fail you, neither will He forsake you.

JULY 29TH

TRANSFORMATIONAL MEDITATIONS

"Scripture for the Day"
Luke Chapters 23-24

PHRASE OF THE DAY

If you don't know who you are, you will try to imitate others, and you will become a victim of other people's opinions, and that means they possess your life. Discover your best self by meditating on God's Word.

Daily Prayer

_____

_____

_____

_____

_____

JULY 30TH

TRANSFORMATIONAL MEDITATIONS

Daily Prayer

_____

_____

_____

_____

_____

"Scripture for the Day"
1st Thessalonians Chapters 4-5

PHRASE OF THE DAY

It's not that some people have willpower and some don't, it's that some people are ready to change and others aren't. Are you ready to be transformed? Surrender to God today.

JULY 31ST

TRANSFORMATIONAL MEDITATIONS

"Scripture for the Day"
Leviticus Chapters 22-24

PHRASE OF THE DAY

Being carnal is not just a problem for unbelievers, it's an outlook we have to change by renewing our minds.

Daily Prayer

_____

_____

_____

_____

_____

AUGUST 1ST

TRANSFORMATIONAL MEDITATIONS

Daily Prayer

_____

_____

_____

_____

_____

"Scripture for the Day"
2nd Kings Chapters 21-25

_____

PHRASE OF THE DAY

When your ways meet up with God's way, you can
either change your way by seeking understanding
through Him or stay in bondage to sin and death.

AUGUST 2ND

TRANSFORMATIONAL MEDITATIONS

"Scripture for the Day"
Psalm Chapters 90-92

PHRASE OF THE DAY

A seed has all it needs inside to fulfill its purpose. A
seed must die to itself once it is planted in order to
grow. Your destiny is being nurtured by trials.

Daily Prayer

AUGUST 3RD

TRANSFORMATIONAL MEDITATIONS

Daily Prayer

_____

_____

_____

_____

_____

"Scripture for the Day"
Proverbs Chapters 14-15

PHRASE OF THE DAY

Life is about choices, so you are in charge of how your day will go. Life or death? On purpose, I choose life! The enemy's warfare is in the mind; we must renew it and overcome.

AUGUST 4TH

TRANSFORMATIONAL MEDITATIONS

"Scripture for the Day"
Ezekiel Chapters 43-48

PHRASE OF THE DAY

Remember that no matter what may come your way, you can do all things through Christ who strengthens you.

Daily Prayer

_____

_____

_____

_____

_____

AUGUST 5TH

TRANSFORMATIONAL MEDITATIONS

Daily Prayer

_____

_____

_____

_____

_____

"Scripture for the Day"
John Chapters 1-2

PHRASE OF THE DAY

Many of us are wounded in spiritual warfare, not because
Jesus hasn't given us power, but rather because we don't
live, truly repentive lives, based on the cross. Love is light.

AUGUST 6TH

TRANSFORMATIONAL MEDITATIONS

"Scripture for the Day"
2nd Thessalonians

PHRASE OF THE DAY

When you put your hope in the Lord, your strength
will be renewed. According to the Word of God, you
will also soar on wings like eagles; you will run and
not grow weary; you will walk and not faint.

Daily Prayer

_____

_____

_____

_____

_____

AUGUST 7TH

TRANSFORMATIONAL MEDITATIONS

Daily Prayer

_____

_____

_____

_____

_____

"Scripture for the Day"
Leviticus Chapters 25-27

PHRASE OF THE DAY

Without love we are just dry bones,
making a lot of irritating noise.

AUGUST 8TH

TRANSFORMATIONAL MEDITATIONS

"Scripture for the Day"
1st Chronicles Chapters 1-4

PHRASE OF THE DAY

Be sincere in all that you do, and speak the truth. Do not be double minded. Let your yes be yes and your no, be no.

Daily Prayer

_____

_____

_____

_____

_____

AUGUST 9TH

TRANSFORMATIONAL MEDITATIONS

Daily Prayer

_____

_____

_____

_____

_____

"Scripture for the Day"
Psalm Chapters 93-95

PHRASE OF THE DAY

Human nature hides or overlooks our mistakes and sins.
It's hard to learn from a mistake you don't acknowledge
making. Everyone makes mistakes, learn and grow.

AUGUST 10TH

TRANSFORMATIONAL MEDITATIONS

"Scripture for the Day"
Proverbs Chapter 16

PHRASE OF THE DAY

When we confess our sins and pray for others, we are healed in many ways. Have you prayed for someone else yet, today?

Daily Prayer

_____

_____

_____

_____

_____

AUGUST 11TH

TRANSFORMATIONAL MEDITATIONS

Daily Prayer

_____

_____

_____

_____

_____

"Scripture for the Day"
Daniel Chapters 1-6

PHRASE OF THE DAY

God freely gave you the gift that keeps on giving, Jesus.
So don't you stop giving, you can't out give the Father.

AUGUST 12TH

TRANSFORMATIONAL MEDITATIONS

"Scripture for the Day"
John Chapters 3-4

PHRASE OF THE DAY

Today, I want you to know that God is always with you. He is a Mighty Warrior who takes great delight in you. God will rejoice over you with singing. Bless and praise His holy name.

Daily Prayer

_____

_____

_____

_____

_____

AUGUST 13TH

TRANSFORMATIONAL MEDITATIONS

Daily Prayer

_____

_____

_____

_____

_____

"Scripture for the Day"
1st Timothy Chapters 1-3

PHRASE OF THE DAY

For some, the two most difficult sins to resist are pride and sexual immortality. Pride says I deserve it, and sexual desires say I need it. Drunkenness just covers it up. Ask God to search and heal your heart.

AUGUST 14TH

TRANSFORMATIONAL MEDITATIONS

"Scripture for the Day"
Numbers Chapters 1-4

PHRASE OF THE DAY

The Word of God says that if we love God, we will keep His commandments. If we are not keeping God's commandments, then we need to ask God to help us to love Him more.

Daily Prayer

_____

_____

_____

_____

_____

AUGUST 15TH

TRANSFORMATIONAL MEDITATIONS

Daily Prayer

_____

_____

_____

_____

_____

"Scripture for the Day"
1st Chronicles Chapters 5-9

PHRASE OF THE DAY

A believer will backslide when they do not function
in their gifting or calling. Ask God for strength
to resist the tempation to use His gifts for your
own benefit, but rather to protect and serve.

AUGUST 16TH

TRANSFORMATIONAL MEDITATIONS

"Scripture for the Day"
Psalm Chapters 96-98

PHRASE OF THE DAY

Gentleness and self-control have no law against
them. When you live for Christ, you will
live a life that goes against the grain.

Daily Prayer

_____

_____

_____

_____

_____

AUGUST 17TH

TRANSFORMATIONAL MEDITATIONS

Daily Prayer

_____

_____

_____

_____

_____

"Scripture for the Day"
Proverbs Chapters 17-18

PHRASE OF THE DAY

Once you are saved, that's when the work begins. You have to develop a relationship with God, as this is your part of the job. You must, on a daily basis, join together your heart, your dreams, your goals, your thoughts, and characteristics until they become one with the Father.

AUGUST 18TH

TRANSFORMATIONAL MEDITATIONS

"Scripture for the Day"
Daniel Chapters 7-12

PHRASE OF THE DAY

Respect your elders and humble yourself, for pride is not of God. God opposes the proud but He gives grace to the humble.

Daily Prayer

_____

_____

_____

_____

_____

AUGUST 19TH

TRANSFORMATIONAL MEDITATIONS

Daily Prayer

_____

_____

_____

_____

_____

"Scripture for the Day"
John Chapters 5-6

PHRASE OF THE DAY

If we are to truly follow Christ, we must deny ourselves, pick up our cross and follow Him daily. Christianity is not church on Sundays, rather, it is a lifestyle, a daily walk with God.

AUGUST 20TH

TRANSFORMATIONAL MEDITATIONS

"Scripture for the Day"
1st Timothy Chapters 4-6

PHRASE OF THE DAY

I am the bread of life; he who comes to me will not hunger, and he who believes in me will never thirst John 6:35 … and everyone who lives and believes in Me will never die. Say it with me, I shall live and not die, in Jesus name, amen!

Daily Prayer

_____

_____

_____

_____

_____

AUGUST 21ST

TRANSFORMATIONAL MEDITATIONS

Daily Prayer

_____

_____

_____

_____

"Scripture for the Day"
Numbers Chapters 5-8

PHRASE OF THE DAY

You have heard the saying, "Treat others the way that you would like to be treated." Let us go a little bit further. Has God been patient with you? Has God been kind to you? Has our Lord God forgiven you for all of your sins and been merciful towards you? Let us also be kind. Let us also be merciful and forgiving and patient towards others also then. Amen.

AUGUST 22ND

TRANSFORMATIONAL MEDITATIONS

"Scripture for the Day"
1st Chronicles Chapters 10-14

PHRASE OF THE DAY

If anyone is dealing with any kind of fear today, we need you to bind it right now with the blood of Jesus. Tell fear farewell, goodbye, be gone forever! Then say hello to Grace.

Daily Prayer

_____

_____

_____

_____

_____

AUGUST 23RD

TRANSFORMATIONAL MEDITATIONS

Daily Prayer

_____

_____

_____

_____

_____

"Scripture for the Day"
Psalm Chapters 99-101

PHRASE OF THE DAY

Do we have any radical believers that will pray
for God's kingdom to come on Earth as it is in
Heaven and have the faith to walk it out?

AUGUST 24TH

TRANSFORMATIONAL MEDITATIONS

"Scripture for the Day"
Proverbs Chapter 19

PHRASE OF THE DAY

As Believers, we are instructed to trust in the Lord with all of
our heart and to lean not on our own understanding. We are to
submit to Him in all of our ways and He will direct our paths.
God is not a man that He should lie.
God never fails.

Daily Prayer

_____

_____

_____

_____

_____

AUGUST 25TH

TRANSFORMATIONAL MEDITATIONS

Daily Prayer

_____

_____

_____

_____

_____

"Scripture for the Day"
Hosea Chapters 1-7

PHRASE OF THE DAY

Clothe yourselves with compassion, kindness, humility,
gentleness, and patience. Forgive as the Lord has
forgiven you, and over all these virtues put on love,
which binds them all together in perfect unity.

AUGUST 26TH

TRANSFORMATIONAL MEDITATIONS

"Scripture for the Day"
John Chapters 7-9

PHRASE OF THE DAY

God's timing can be different than ours. He knows when we are ready and is aware of the moments when we are not. God will restore you. He will make you strong, firm, and steadfast.

Daily Prayer

_____

_____

_____

_____

_____

AUGUST 27TH

TRANSFORMATIONAL MEDITATIONS

Daily Prayer

_____

_____

_____

_____

_____

"Scripture for the Day"
2nd Timothy Chapters 1-2

PHRASE OF THE DAY

I decree and I declare that the joy of the Lord is my
strength, so I will be joyful in hope, patient in affliction
and faithful in prayer, in the name of Jesus.

AUGUST 28TH

TRANSFORMATIONAL MEDITATIONS

"Scripture for the Day"
Numbers Chapters 9-12

PHRASE OF THE DAY

When we are offended by friends and family, it is
easy to sharpen our tongue with anger and bitterness.
Even though information may be true and accurate,
motives are impure. When we sow discord or separation
among brethren, it is an abomination to the Lord.

Daily Prayer

_____

_____

_____

_____

_____

AUGUST 29TH

TRANSFORMATIONAL MEDITATIONS

Daily Prayer

_____

_____

_____

_____

_____

"Scripture for the Day"
1st Chronicles Chapters 15-19

PHRASE OF THE DAY

Lord, You are my Fortress, my Rock and
my Salvation, I will not be shaken.

AUGUST 30TH

TRANSFORMATIONAL MEDITATIONS

"Scripture for the Day"
Psalm Chapters 102-104

PHRASE OF THE DAY

Weight is like sin, it's easy to gain and hard to lose.
Everyone is looking for that magic weight loss or no
sin pill, but sweat and hard work are required.

Daily Prayer

_____

_____

_____

_____

_____

AUGUST 31ST

TRANSFORMATIONAL MEDITATIONS

Daily Prayer

_____

_____

_____

_____

_____

"Scripture for the Day"
Proverbs Chapters 20-21

_____

PHRASE OF THE DAY

Thank You Heavenly Father for removing our transgression from us as far as the east is from the west. What an Amazing and Mighty God we serve.

SEPTEMBER 1ST

TRANSFORMATIONAL MEDITATIONS

"Scripture for the Day"
Hosea Chapters 8-14

PHRASE OF THE DAY

God, You are more powerful than my past. My
future is safe and secure in Your hands.

Daily Prayer

_____

_____

_____

_____

_____

SEPTEMBER 2ND

TRANSFORMATIONAL MEDITATIONS

Daily Prayer

_____

_____

_____

_____

_____

"Scripture for the Day"
John Chapters 10-12

_____

PHRASE OF THE DAY

God will deal with you on how you treat others, not
how others treat you. Get this in your soul.

SEPTEMBER 3RD

TRANSFORMATIONAL MEDITATIONS

"Scripture for the Day"
2 Timothy Chapters 3-4

PHRASE OF THE DAY

Our relationship with God comes from our faith and trust in Him. Our own understanding contradicts our trust in God.

Daily Prayer

SEPTEMBER 4TH

TRANSFORMATIONAL MEDITATIONS

Daily Prayer

_____

_____

_____

_____

_____

"Scripture for the Day"
Numbers Chapters 13-16

PHRASE OF THE DAY

The body of Christ is suffering from identity crisis. If we don't know who and who's we are, when the trial shows up, we fold. The battle is not yours but God's.

SEPTEMBER 5TH

TRANSFORMATIONAL MEDITATIONS

"Scripture for the Day"
1st Chronicles Chapters 20-24

PHRASE OF THE DAY

Ever wonder why some people are so hateful? It's because they don't know and trust the Lord. Try waking up each morning thanking God and putting on an armor of love and compassion.

Daily Prayer

_____

_____

_____

_____

_____

SEPTEMBER 6TH

TRANSFORMATIONAL MEDITATIONS

Daily Prayer

_____

_____

_____

_____

_____

"Scripture for the Day"
Psalm Chapters 105-107

PHRASE OF THE DAY

In order to have lasting victories in our lives, our soul must
be fixed on Jesus rather than focused on our failures.

SEPTEMBER 7TH

TRANSFORMATIONAL MEDITATIONS

"Scripture for the Day"
Proverbs Chapter 22

PHRASE OF THE DAY

John 10:27-30 Don't let the devil shake your salvation today. You are saved by the grace of God through faith in Jesus Christ. Believers are secured.

If you need a visual on why you should not be sick, watch The Passion of Christ, look at the stripes He took so that you would not be ill. Remind sickness and those demonic spirits of those stripes and that Jesus freed you from them. Jesus took on all and gave it back to Satan where it came from.

Daily Prayer

_____

_____

_____

_____

_____

SEPTEMBER 8TH

TRANSFORMATIONAL MEDITATIONS

Daily Prayer

_____

_____

_____

_____

_____

"Scripture for the Day"
The Book of Joel

PHRASE OF THE DAY

God's power is in His Love. You can't have His love
without forgiveness. Many people today are walking around
with unforgiveness and no power. Forgive and live!

SEPTEMBER 9TH

TRANSFORMATIONAL MEDITATIONS

"Scripture for the Day"
John Chapters 13-15

PHRASE OF THE DAY

If you have three different personalities, church, work, and
home, you are a bleeding Christian. The church should be
like a hospital, if you tell them your symptoms, they give
you what you need to get rid of the illness. The church
has an issue of blood, act like it and search for Jesus the
cure. If you are in a hospital (church) that doesn't have
the cure you need to press on to find the Cure (Jesus).

Daily Prayer

_____

_____

_____

_____

_____

SEPTEMBER 10TH

TRANSFORMATIONAL MEDITATIONS

Daily Prayer

_____

_____

_____

_____

_____

"Scripture for the Day"
The Book of Titus

_____

PHRASE OF THE DAY

I don't care what you are going through, you can't quit.
The key words are, going through. You are not in park,
keep moving. God is able so encourage someone today.

SEPTEMBER 11TH

TRANSFORMATIONAL MEDITATIONS

"Scripture for the Day"
Numbers Chapters 17-20

PHRASE OF THE DAY

Intimacy was given by God to help express love, not to create it. People are looking for intimacy without love, love without marriage, and marriage without responsibility.

Daily Prayer

SEPTEMBER 12TH

TRANSFORMATIONAL MEDITATIONS

Daily Prayer

_____

_____

_____

_____

_____

"Scripture for the Day"
1 Chronicles Chapters 25-29

PHRASE OF THE DAY

Why is it that people have to hit rock bottom before
they can come to Christ? Seek God daily.

SEPTEMBER 13TH

TRANSFORMATIONAL MEDITATIONS

"Scripture for the Day"
Psalm Chapters 108-110

PHRASE OF THE DAY

What comes out of the mouth defiles man. We only speak
what's on our heart. If your heart hurts, you will hurt others.
If that's you repent and let Jesus heal your heart today.

Daily Prayer

_____

_____

_____

_____

_____

SEPTEMBER 14TH

TRANSFORMATIONAL MEDITATIONS

Daily Prayer

_____

_____

_____

_____

_____

"Scripture for the Day"
Proverbs Chapters 23-24

PHRASE OF THE DAY

A true leader does not suppress, oppress, or depress
the potential and talents of others. He provides an
environment to release and cultivate their gifts.

SEPTEMBER 15TH

TRANSFORMATIONAL MEDITATIONS

"Scripture for the Day"
Amos Chapters 1-4

PHRASE OF THE DAY

We are servants before we are leaders. Once we are
spiritually mature, we become friends of Jesus. Being
friends with Jesus means dying to selfish motives.

Daily Prayer

_____

_____

_____

_____

_____

SEPTEMBER 16TH

TRANSFORMATIONAL MEDITATIONS

Daily Prayer

_____

_____

_____

_____

_____

"Scripture for the Day"
John Chapters 16-18

PHRASE OF THE DAY

Do not be overcome by evil but overcome evil with good.
The best way to get rid of enemies is to turn them into
friends. Encourage someone today, in Jesus' name.

SEPTEMBER 17TH

TRANSFORMATIONAL MEDITATIONS

"Scripture for the Day"
The Book of Philemon

PHRASE OF THE DAY

Saints trust God and stop asking "why you're going through?"
Just embrace your valley and learn, you will need that lesson
at your next level in Him. Encourage someone today.

Daily Prayer

_____

_____

_____

_____

_____

SEPTEMBER 18TH

TRANSFORMATIONAL MEDITATIONS

Daily Prayer

_____

_____

_____

_____

_____

"Scripture for the Day"
Numbers Chapters 21-24

PHRASE OF THE DAY

Time for preaching is over. People need to be taught about
spiritual things. All the preaching in the world won't keep
a demon out of your house or your families bloodline.
Most demonic presence is caused by the words and
actions of the individual. Jesus died for us to have power
over the demonic, but if we are not taught that, we will
continue to have fornication, drug & other addictions,
low self-esteem, hatred, condemnation, poverty stricken,
and drunkards and envious people running the house.

SEPTEMBER 19TH

TRANSFORMATIONAL MEDITATIONS

"Scripture for the Day"
2 Chronicles Chapters 1-5

PHRASE OF THE DAY

The enemies' strongest weapon is deception, but the might
of the truth will set you free. Walking in the flesh is bondage,
walking in the spirit is freedom. Read Colossians 3:5

Daily Prayer

SEPTEMBER 20TH

TRANSFORMATIONAL MEDITATIONS

Daily Prayer

_____

_____

_____

_____

_____

"Scripture for the Day"
Psalm Chapters 111-113

PHRASE OF THE DAY

Remember when the pigs drowned themselves when Jesus allowed the legion (spirits) to enter them? We are smarter than a bunch of pigs, right? By seeking God, He will not allow fear and doubt or demons to have their way with us.

SEPTEMBER 21ST

TRANSFORMATIONAL MEDITATIONS

"Scripture for the Day"
Proverbs Chapter 25

PHRASE OF THE DAY

Leaning is the sense of putting your full weight on
something, resting and trusting that person or thing. When
we have an important decision to make, sometimes we
feel we can't trust anyone not even God. Remember,
God knows what's best for all of us. Bring your decisions
to God in prayer and follow His lead. Amen.

Daily Prayer

_____

_____

_____

_____

_____

SEPTEMBER 22ND

TRANSFORMATIONAL MEDITATIONS

Daily Prayer

_____

_____

_____

_____

_____

"Scripture for the Day"
Amos Chapters 5-9

PHRASE OF THE DAY

People give up too easy these days, read Matthew 7:7-12.
Jesus tells us to be persistent in seeking God. Continue
to ask for patience, knowledge, wisdom and love.

SEPTEMBER 23RD

TRANSFORMATIONAL MEDITATIONS

"Scripture for the Day"
John Chapters 19-21

PHRASE OF THE DAY

When we neglect to teach our people God's ways, then we abandon them to the ways of the world. We can't tell someone not to curse while cursing, lead by example.

Daily Prayer

_____

_____

_____

_____

_____

SEPTEMBER 24TH

TRANSFORMATIONAL MEDITATIONS

Daily Prayer

_____

_____

_____

_____

_____

"Scripture for the Day"
Hebrews Chapters 1-4

PHRASE OF THE DAY

I decree that no weapon that is formed against your marriage
(spiritually or physically) shall be able to prosper against
you in any way. And every word that is spoken against you
shall fall to the ground. For this is the heritage that you have
as a servant of the Lord, and your righteousness is of Him.
Read Isaiah 54:17.

SEPTEMBER 25TH

TRANSFORMATIONAL MEDITATIONS

"Scripture for the Day"
Numbers Chapters 25-28

PHRASE OF THE DAY

Whatever trial you are going through, is the vehicle God is using to get you to your blessing. Do not get out of the vehicle until you are at your destination.

Daily Prayer

_____

_____

_____

_____

_____

SEPTEMBER 26TH

TRANSFORMATIONAL MEDITATIONS

Daily Prayer

_____

_____

_____

_____

_____

"Scripture for the Day"
2nd Chronicles Chapters 6-10

PHRASE OF THE DAY

Those who have buried their gift, dig it up now and
take off the grave clothes. While you are there, put
down those grave clothes of fear and bury it.
Faith is alive!

SEPTEMBER 27TH

TRANSFORMATIONAL MEDITATIONS

"Scripture for the Day"
Psalm Chapters 114-116

PHRASE OF THE DAY

Romans 13:8-10, Love does not harm. If this is so, we will not lie, steal, covet, murder, nor do anything else God tells us not to do. The same way we want the best for ourselves, we should give our best. Givers rarely suffer from low self-esteem. If we obey the law of love, it supersedes religious and civil laws.

Daily Prayer

_____

_____

_____

_____

_____

SEPTEMBER 28TH

TRANSFORMATIONAL MEDITATIONS

Daily Prayer

_____

_____

_____

_____

_____

"Scripture for the Day"
Proverbs Chapters 26-27

PHRASE OF THE DAY

Waiting on God is not easy. Often it seems that He isn't answering our prayers or doesn't understand the urgency of the situation. That kind of thinking implies that God is not in control. Waiting produces patients and when patients is fully grown you will lack nothing. God is worth waiting for. Amen.

SEPTEMBER 29TH

TRANSFORMATIONAL MEDITATIONS

"Scripture for the Day"
The Book of Obadiah

PHRASE OF THE DAY

Whoever corrects a mocker invites insult, whoever rebukes a wicked man incurs abuse. Do not rebuke a mocker or he will hate you. Rebuke a wiseman and he will love you. Are you a mocker or a wiseman? You can tell by the way you respond to criticism. Will you be angry and respond with *"You can't judge me."*, or will you thank God for sending correction? If a person were to bless you with your rent money, it would be easy for you to say and believe that God sent him, right? What if he comes to you saying, *"Stop shacking up."*, would be quick to say that God did not send him? God chasens those He loves. He corrects His children. Are you a child of God? Then learn to accept correction.

Daily Prayer

_____

_____

_____

_____

_____

SEPTEMBER 30TH

TRANSFORMATIONAL MEDITATIONS

Daily Prayer

_____

_____

_____

_____

_____

"Scripture for the Day"
Acts Chapters 1-2

PHRASE OF THE DAY

If you pull a fish out of water or a plant out of the
dirt they will eventually die because it is separated
from its life source. Sin separates us from God.
Feeding on His Word sustains our life.

OCTOBER 1ST

TRANSFORMATIONAL MEDITATIONS

"Scripture for the Day"
Hebrews Chapters 5-7

PHRASE OF THE DAY

There is so much deception (Satan) in the world. I think most people want to do right but are taught wrong. I hear God saying, "Who told you that?" Pray for wisdom, so that you can more easily spot a wolf in sheep's clothing.

Daily Prayer

_____

_____

_____

_____

_____

OCTOBER 2ND

TRANSFORMATIONAL MEDITATIONS

Daily Prayer

_____

_____

_____

_____

_____

"Scripture for the Day"
Numbers Chapters 29-32

PHRASE OF THE DAY

Ask God to search your heart and bring to light anything
that is dark. He will send someone to touch that sore.
Thank God and receive correction (healing) in that area.

OCTOBER 3RD

TRANSFORMATIONAL MEDITATIONS

"Scripture for the Day"
2nd Chronicles Chapters 11-15

PHRASE OF THE DAY

The truth needs no justification, but a lie cannot operate without many excuses. It's ok not to know or have to explain everything, lies however are wrapped in explanations.

Daily Prayer

_____

_____

_____

_____

_____

OCTOBER 4TH

TRANSFORMATIONAL MEDITATIONS

Daily Prayer

_____

_____

_____

_____

_____

"Scripture for the Day"
Psalm Chapters 117-118

PHRASE OF THE DAY

To transform is to change in appearance. When you do the
Word of God, people will increasingly acknowledge and
compliment the positive changes in your appearance.

OCTOBER 5TH

TRANSFORMATIONAL MEDITATIONS

"Scripture for the Day"
Proverbs Chapter 28

PHRASE OF THE DAY

There is a big difference in being conceived and being born again. When a child is conceived there is evidence meaning that they see, smell, hear, and feel the things of this world. So, if someone is born again into the spiritual world, there ought to be evidence that they should see, smell, hear, and feel in that world.

Daily Prayer

_____

_____

_____

_____

_____

OCTOBER 6TH

TRANSFORMATIONAL MEDITATIONS

Daily Prayer

_____

_____

_____

_____

_____

"Scripture for the Day"
The Book of Jonah
_____

PHRASE OF THE DAY

Praise is what I do even when I'm going through; I
lift my hands in praise. I praise Him through the good
and the bad, through the happy or sad. Amen.

OCTOBER 7TH

TRANSFORMATIONAL MEDITATIONS

"Scripture for the Day"
Acts Chapters 3-4

PHRASE OF THE DAY

If you escape corruption of the world by knowing our Lord and Savior Jesus Christ, stay focused on His Word so that you will not once again get entangled in things that are immoral.

Daily Prayer

_____

_____

_____

_____

_____

OCTOBER 8TH

TRANSFORMATIONAL MEDITATIONS

Daily Prayer

_____

_____

_____

_____

_____

"Scripture for the Day"
Hebrews Chapters 8-10

PHRASE OF THE DAY

Listen my son to your father's instruction and do not forsake
your mother's teachings. Proverbs 1:8. This tells me that the
world is doing it wrong. Too many parents these days are
depending on the schools and churches to guide their children
when it's the parents job. Parents, learn God's teachings
so that you can instruct them in the ways of the Lord.

OCTOBER 9TH

TRANSFORMATIONAL MEDITATIONS

"Scripture for the Day"
Numbers Chapters 33-36

PHRASE OF THE DAY

When you live for the will of God, you will not fulfill
worldly desires. As a result, you WILL suffer in the flesh,
Jesus suffered great hostility from religious people.

Daily Prayer

_____

_____

_____

_____

_____

OCTOBER 10TH

TRANSFORMATIONAL MEDITATIONS

Daily Prayer

_____

_____

_____

_____

_____

"Scripture for the Day"
2nd Chronicles Chapters 16-20

PHRASE OF THE DAY

Our source of life is clearly our Heavenly Father, so
why receive instruction on how to live from anywhere
else? Be compelled to seek only His counsel.

OCTOBER 11TH

TRANSFORMATIONAL MEDITATIONS

"Scripture for the Day"
Psalm Chapter 119

PHRASE OF THE DAY

No man can shut what you open, no one can open what
you shut. The power is in the tongue. What are you
releasing into the atmosphere? Change your confessions.
When you get promoted in the world you get more
benefits but do less work. It's the same in the spirit world,
your maturity in God is rewarded with less work.

Daily Prayer

OCTOBER 12TH

TRANSFORMATIONAL MEDITATIONS

Daily Prayer

_____

_____

_____

_____

_____

"Scripture for the Day"
Proverbs Chapters 29-30

PHRASE OF THE DAY

I don't know what you are going through right now, but
what I do know is we have been given authority. Get up
NOW, out of your situation and walk toward Jesus, Amen.

OCTOBER 13TH

TRANSFORMATIONAL MEDITATIONS

"Scripture for the Day"
The Book of Micah

PHRASE OF THE DAY

If we stand in the storms, our root system (faith)
goes deeper into our source. We should not resist
the very thing that God sends to mature us.
Trust the Lord.

Daily Prayer

_____

_____

_____

_____

_____

OCTOBER 14TH

TRANSFORMATIONAL MEDITATIONS

Daily Prayer

_____

_____

_____

_____

_____

"Scripture for the Day"
Acts Chapters 5-6

PHRASE OF THE DAY

Two can't walk together unless they agree. When two or more agree, it is established. We need to come out of agreement with death and walk into agreement with the Word of God.

OCTOBER 15TH

TRANSFORMATIONAL MEDITATIONS

"Scripture for the Day"
Hebrews Chapters 11-13

PHRASE OF THE DAY

I saw a pit bull dragging something on a track. The Spirt of the Lord spoke to me and said this is what most people allow their flesh to do, drag them. We must train our flesh so it will not control us, the same way we trained our flesh to smoke and drink. Our body rejected these things when we first started, but we kept going (trained). Our body is our temple, let it be a sacrifice to the Most High.

Daily Prayer

OCTOBER 16TH

TRANSFORMATIONAL MEDITATIONS

Daily Prayer

_____

_____

_____

_____

_____

"Scripture for the Day"
Deuteronomy Chapters 1-3

PHRASE OF THE DAY

Don't be deceived, God is not mocked. He said in His own
Word that He loves you and will never leave you nor forsake
you. So don't you leave Him; your will can't be breached.

OCTOBER 17TH

TRANSFORMATIONAL MEDITATIONS

"Scripture for the Day"
2nd Chronicles Chapters 21-24

PHRASE OF THE DAY

All authority in Heaven has been given to you,
therefore go and make disciples. Baptize them in
the name of the Father, Son, and Holy Spirit. Teach
them to obey the teaching of the Lord our God.

Daily Prayer

OCTOBER 18TH

TRANSFORMATIONAL MEDITATIONS

Daily Prayer

_____

_____

_____

_____

_____

"Scripture for the Day"
Psalm Chapters 120-121

PHRASE OF THE DAY

Jesus modeled how to submit to the Father. He only
did what He saw His Father do. What are your children
(spiritually or naturally) doing? Pick your leaders wisely.

OCTOBER 19TH

TRANSFORMATIONAL MEDITATIONS

"Scripture for the Day"
Proverbs Chapter 31

PHRASE OF THE DAY

Whenever two agree on a thing it is established. We have
to agree to be deceived (mislead, tricked, betray, lied
to, conned, misinformed, ripped off). All deception is
dealing with lack of knowledge of the truth. Jesus came
to set the captives free; so, seek Him in all that you do.

Daily Prayer

_____

_____

_____

_____

_____

OCTOBER 20TH

TRANSFORMATIONAL MEDITATIONS

Daily Prayer

_____

_____

_____

_____

_____

"Scripture for the Day"
The Book of Nahum

PHRASE OF THE DAY

False teaching always caters to the needs of the flesh, but
seeking Truth (God) can heal the mind, body and soul.

OCTOBER 21ST

TRANSFORMATIONAL MEDITATIONS

"Scripture for the Day"
Acts Chapters 7-8

PHRASE OF THE DAY

Read Matthew 16. When you walk with revelation knowledge
you are not selfish, but Kingdom minded. In that walk,
God will allow you to bind and loose with His keys.

Daily Prayer

_____

_____

_____

_____

_____

OCTOBER 22ND

TRANSFORMATIONAL MEDITATIONS

Daily Prayer

_____

_____

_____

_____

_____

"Scripture for the Day"
James Chapters 1-3

PHRASE OF THE DAY

The Spirit of the Lord is on me, for He has anointed
me to teach the gospel in a way that would open
the eyes of the blind and set the captives free.

OCTOBER 23RD

TRANSFORMATIONAL MEDITATIONS

"Scripture for the Day"
Deuteronomy Chapters 4-6

PHRASE OF THE DAY

The same way you would not brew new water through an old coffee filter, we have to renew our mind to effectively receive the Word that produces power.

Daily Prayer

_____

_____

_____

_____

_____

OCTOBER 24TH

TRANSFORMATIONAL MEDITATIONS

Daily Prayer

_____

_____

_____

_____

_____

"Scripture for the Day"
2nd Chronicles Chapters 25-28

PHRASE OF THE DAY

If you try to save your physical life from death, pain, or discomfort, on your own, you may lose your life to fear. When we give our lives over to Christ, it produces faith.

OCTOBER 25TH

TRANSFORMATIONAL MEDITATIONS

"Scripture for the Day"
Psalm Chapters 122-124

PHRASE OF THE DAY

You cannot make a withdrawal where there is
no deposit. If you never put God's Word in, it
is impossible for His Word to come out.

Daily Prayer

OCTOBER 26TH

TRANSFORMATIONAL MEDITATIONS

Daily Prayer

_____

_____

_____

_____

_____

"Scripture for the Day"
Ecclesiastes Chapters 1-2

PHRASE OF THE DAY

Bitterness is a root. If roots are nursed, watered, protected, fed, and given attention, they increase in depth and strength. Roots are hard to pull up. Produce sweet roots by watering yourself with the Word of God.

OCTOBER 27TH

TRANSFORMATIONAL MEDITATIONS

"Scripture for the Day"
The Book of Habakkuk

PHRASE OF THE DAY

I dare you to praise God for whatever or whoever
has you going through. We are hard pressed on every
side but not crushed, perplexed but not in despair,
persecuted but not abandoned, struck down but not
destroyed. We always carry around the death of
Jesus, so that the life of Jesus may be revealed.

Daily Prayer

OCTOBER 28TH

TRANSFORMATIONAL MEDITATIONS

Daily Prayer

_____

_____

_____

_____

_____

"Scripture for the Day"
Acts Chapters 9-10

PHRASE OF THE DAY

Jesus is the author and finisher of our faith. Jesus initiated, generated, produced, upheld, and sustains the salvation of all mankind. He is the sole source of our redemption. So, start acting like it and be grateful, and pass on a blessing today.

OCTOBER 29TH

TRANSFORMATIONAL MEDITATIONS

"Scripture for the Day"
James Chapters 4-5

PHRASE OF THE DAY

Our attitude towards others reflects our relationship with God. Anger is a dangerous emotion that can leap out of control, leading to violence, mental stress and spiritual damage. Read Matthew 5:21-26.

Daily Prayer

_____

_____

_____

_____

_____

OCTOBER 30TH

TRANSFORMATIONAL MEDITATIONS

Daily Prayer

_____

_____

_____

_____

_____

"Scripture for the Day"
Deuteronomy Chapters 7-9

PHRASE OF THE DAY

Our will is a powerful weapon. If your heart is
hardened your will, will oppose God's will. Please
use your will to come closer to God by seeking
His face no matter what the circumstance.

OCTOBER 31ST

TRANSFORMATIONAL MEDITATIONS

"Scripture for the Day"
2nd Chronicles Chapters 29-32

PHRASE OF THE DAY

A lie needs the support of an excuse, but
the Truth stands on its own.

Daily Prayer

_____

_____

_____

_____

_____

NOVEMBER 1ST

TRANSFORMATIONAL MEDITATIONS

Daily Prayer

_____

_____

_____

_____

_____

"Scripture for the Day"
Psalm Chapters 125-127

PHRASE OF THE DAY

If you have no power in your prayer, it's because of Mark
11:24-25. Quit lying to yourself and break free from bondage
to anger and fear. God moves on faith and compassion.

NOVEMBER 2ND

TRANSFORMATIONAL MEDITATIONS

"Scripture for the Day"
Ecclesiastes Chapters 3-4

PHRASE OF THE DAY

Give me that joy I can't explain and that peace that
won't let me complain. Give that love that will never
change. Humble yourself to change your ways.

Daily Prayer

_____

_____

_____

_____

_____

NOVEMBER 3RD

TRANSFORMATIONAL MEDITATIONS

Daily Prayer

_____

_____

_____

_____

_____

"Scripture for the Day"
The Book of Zephaniah

PHRASE OF THE DAY

It is extremely difficult to do something that you know nothing about. First knowledge is required, then practicing that which you have learnt, which will lead to understanding.

NOVEMBER 4TH

TRANSFORMATIONAL MEDITATIONS

"Scripture for the Day"
Acts Chapters 11-12

PHRASE OF THE DAY

We look at what we do as something we can't help, but
we only get good at what we practice. We also know
the difference between right and not right. Repent.

Daily Prayer

_____

_____

_____

_____

_____

NOVEMBER 5TH

TRANSFORMATIONAL MEDITATIONS

Daily Prayer

_____

_____

_____

_____

_____

"Scripture for the Day"
1st Peter Chapters 1-3

PHRASE OF THE DAY

We are taught to put off our former way of life, which
was corrupted by its deceitful desires, in order to be made
new in attitude and mind in Christ Jesus, Ephesians 4.

NOVEMBER 6TH

TRANSFORMATIONAL MEDITATIONS

"Scripture for the Day"
Deuteronomy Chapters 10-12

PHRASE OF THE DAY

Curse is the result of being disobedient to God's
Word. To break the curse, repent and obey. Pride
would keep the curse and say all is well.

Daily Prayer

_____

_____

_____

_____

_____

NOVEMBER 7TH

TRANSFORMATIONAL MEDITATIONS

Daily Prayer

_____

_____

_____

_____

_____

"Scripture for the Day"
2nd Chronicles Chapters 33-36

PHRASE OF THE DAY

A transference is about to take place. Before God
separated Egypt from His people, the wealth was
transferred. Saints, receive it in Jesus' name.
Thank you Lord.

TRANSFORMATIONAL MEDITATIONS

"Scripture for the Day"
Psalm Chapters 128-130

PHRASE OF THE DAY

Spiritual food is more than Bible study, prayer, and
attending church; these can be done individually. We
all must do God's will by helping to bring salvation
to completion. We are nourished not only by what
we take in but also by what we give out for God.

Daily Prayer

_____

_____

_____

_____

_____

NOVEMBER 9TH

TRANSFORMATIONAL MEDITATIONS

Daily Prayer

_____

_____

_____

_____

_____

"Scripture for the Day"
Ecclesiastes Chapters 5-6

PHRASE OF THE DAY

You have heard the old saying, "Words will never hurt you", it's a lie, words are fiery darts. Ephesians 4:29, let the words that come out of our mouths produce healing, not sickness.

NOVEMBER 10TH

TRANSFORMATIONAL MEDITATIONS

"Scripture for the Day"
The Book of Haggai

PHRASE OF THE DAY

No weapon formed against you shall prosper, and any
tongue that accuses you shall be found to be wrong.
We sometimes condemn ourselves by speaking
with the old mindset. In other words, give yourself a
chance by renewing your thoughts and speech.

Daily Prayer

_____

_____

_____

_____

_____

NOVEMBER 11TH

TRANSFORMATIONAL MEDITATIONS

Daily Prayer

_____

_____

_____

_____

_____

"Scripture for the Day"
Acts Chapters 13-14

PHRASE OF THE DAY

If you dwell in the secret place of the Most High God,
you shall not fear terror by night, nor arrows that
fly by day. God will deliver and establish you.

NOVEMBER 12TH

TRANSFORMATIONAL MEDITATIONS

"Scripture for the Day"
1 Peter Chapters 4-5

PHRASE OF THE DAY

When you are surrounded by different situations (enemies)
send out the praise team (praise God) and watch your
situations turn on themselves, allowing you to collect the spoil.

Daily Prayer

NOVEMBER 13TH

TRANSFORMATIONAL MEDITATIONS

Daily Prayer

_____

_____

_____

_____

_____

"Scripture for the Day"
Deuteronomy Chapters 13-15

PHRASE OF THE DAY

If you are a believer, your opinion should not override God's Word. God is able to bring you through, without you compromising His Word. I don't have a choice, the Word is my life now, I pray you can say that. Praise God.

NOVEMBER 14TH

TRANSFORMATIONAL MEDITATIONS

"Scripture for the Day"
Ezra Chapters 1-5

PHRASE OF THE DAY

I heard in my spirit a call to rise up, there is supposed to be a big difference between people of the light and people of darkness. You will find what you seek.

Daily Prayer

_____

_____

_____

_____

_____

NOVEMBER 15TH

TRANSFORMATIONAL MEDITATIONS

Daily Prayer

_____

_____

_____

_____

_____

"Scripture for the Day"
Psalm Chapters 131-133

PHRASE OF THE DAY

Religion knows what the Bible says and knows the
teaching, but some do not know Jesus. They are entrenched
in their own system and refuse to let Jesus change
their lives. In Jesus there is love, peace, compassion,
patience, and joy, who would not want to subscribe?

NOVEMBER 16TH

TRANSFORMATIONAL MEDITATIONS

"Scripture for the Day"
Ecclesiastes Chapters 7-8

PHRASE OF THE DAY

Come OUT of agreement with darkness, lying, stealing, cursing, doubt, fear, condemnation, low self-esteem, anger, bitterness, and sexual immorality. Come into agreement with the light, love, peace, joy, longsuffering, meekness, kindness, self-control, and faithfulness. This cannot happen unless you will it.

Daily Prayer

NOVEMBER 17TH

TRANSFORMATIONAL MEDITATIONS

Daily Prayer

_____

_____

_____

_____

_____

"Scripture for the Day"
Zachariah Chapters 1-7

PHRASE OF THE DAY

If you are mentally and physically going through something
right now and you are at your wits end, turn it over to
God. Trust in God's Word, it is for your own good.

NOVEMBER 18TH

TRANSFORMATIONAL MEDITATIONS

"Scripture for the Day"
Acts Chapters 15-16

PHRASE OF THE DAY

Jesus Christ has set us free. Stand firm and don't let yourselves be burdened again by any yoke of slavery.

Daily Prayer

_____

_____

_____

_____

_____

NOVEMBER 19TH

TRANSFORMATIONAL MEDITATIONS

Daily Prayer

_____

_____

_____

_____

_____

"Scripture for the Day"
The Book of 2nd Peter

PHRASE OF THE DAY

Fruit results from planted seeds. When seeds grow,
they bear fruit. Fruit represents outward, visible
behavior. You need to be a fruit inspector.
Look for love.

NOVEMBER 20TH

TRANSFORMATIONAL MEDITATIONS

"Scripture for the Day"
Deuteronomy Chapters 16-19

PHRASE OF THE DAY

Walking in the flesh produces the following bad fruits:
adultery, fornication, lying, hatred, rage, jealousy,
murder, drunkenness, wild living, lust, stealing,
witchcraft, and pride. Walking in the Spirit produces,
love, joy, peace, patience, kindness, goodness,
longsuffering, gentleness, and self-control.
What are you walking in?

Daily Prayer

_____

_____

_____

_____

_____

NOVEMBER 21ST

TRANSFORMATIONAL MEDITATIONS

Daily Prayer

_____

_____

_____

_____

_____

"Scripture for the Day"
Ezra Chapters 6-10

PHRASE OF THE DAY

We can limit what God can do in our lives by assuming
what is impossible. Faith is what moves God, trust
keeps Him steady, belief brings it home.
Lean on God.

NOVEMBER 22ND

TRANSFORMATIONAL MEDITATIONS

"Scripture for the Day"
Psalm Chapters 134-136

PHRASE OF THE DAY

God hears your cry for freedom, but you have to do
something as well. Like the man with the legion, come out
of agreement and throw yourself at the feet of Jesus.

Daily Prayer

_____

_____

_____

_____

_____

NOVEMBER 23RD

TRANSFORMATIONAL MEDITATIONS

Daily Prayer

_____

_____

_____

_____

_____

"Scripture for the Day"
Ecclesiastes Chapters 9-10

PHRASE OF THE DAY

Submission has nothing to do with force. It is an act of
the will. To submit is the choice of the person who is
submitting, not the command of the other, Amen.

NOVEMBER 24TH

TRANSFORMATIONAL MEDITATIONS

"Scripture for the Day"
Zachariah Chapters 8-14

PHRASE OF THE DAY

The test you are experiencing today will
become a testimony tomorrow.

Daily Prayer

_____

_____

_____

_____

_____

TRANSFORMATIONAL MEDITATIONS

Daily Prayer

_____

_____

_____

_____

_____

"Scripture for the Day"
Acts Chapters 17-18

PHRASE OF THE DAY

A thought is not given life until we speak it into existence.
Take control, speak life and if it's not of God speak death to it.

NOVEMBER 26TH

TRANSFORMATIONAL MEDITATIONS

"Scripture for the Day"
1st John Chapters 1-3

PHRASE OF THE DAY

If you are always blaming someone else for your short falls,
then you will never take responsibility for your actions and
will never get help to become the best version of you.

Daily Prayer

_____

_____

_____

_____

_____

NOVEMBER 27TH

TRANSFORMATIONAL MEDITATIONS

Daily Prayer

_____

_____

_____

_____

_____

"Scripture for the Day"
Deuteronomy Chapters 20-22

PHRASE OF THE DAY

You have to be sensitive to the Holy Spirit in this season. He will navigate you to your destiny, just like a good GPS will get you to your destination.

TRANSFORMATIONAL MEDITATIONS

"Scripture for the Day"
Nehemiah Chapters 1-4

PHRASE OF THE DAY

Your situation is not to kill you, but to bring you to
the feet of Jesus. Like a person caught in adultery, let
Jesus intercede (fight) for you. Then sin no more.

Daily Prayer

NOVEMBER 29TH

TRANSFORMATIONAL MEDITATIONS

Daily Prayer

_____

_____

_____

_____

_____

"Scripture for the Day"
Psalm Chapters 137-139

PHRASE OF THE DAY

God gave up all He had to get you and all He asks in return
is for you to trust Him with your all. He said fear not 365
times. Fear does not trust in God nor does it understand Him.

NOVEMBER 30TH

TRANSFORMATIONAL MEDITATIONS

"Scripture for the Day"
Ecclesiastes Chapters 11-12

PHRASE OF THE DAY

Wisdom comes two ways; it is God given or you have to search
for it. There are two kinds of wisdom, Godly and worldly.
Whichever one you have is the one that you searched for.

Daily Prayer

_____

_____

_____

_____

_____

DECEMBER 1ST

TRANSFORMATIONAL MEDITATIONS

Daily Prayer

_____

_____

_____

_____

_____

"Scripture for the Day"
The Book of Malachi

PHRASE OF THE DAY

REAL GROWTH does not take place when you are
reading the Bible or at church. REAL GROWTH
comes from blowing it and realizing what you did!

DECEMBER 2ND

TRANSFORMATIONAL MEDITATIONS

"Scripture for the Day"
Acts Chapters 19-20

PHRASE OF THE DAY

Sin is not only a decision it is a sickness. When you pray
for healing, your answer from God may come in human
form. They will administer God's Word in love.

Daily Prayer

DECEMBER 3RD

TRANSFORMATIONAL MEDITATIONS

Daily Prayer

_____

_____

_____

_____

_____

"Scripture for the Day"
1st John Chapters 4-5

PHRASE OF THE DAY

My friend, take note of this, we all should be quick to
listen, slow to speak and slow to anger. For your anger
does not produce the life God desires for you.

DECEMBER 4TH

TRANSFORMATIONAL MEDITATIONS

"Scripture for the Day"
Deuteronomy Chapters 23-25

PHRASE OF THE DAY

Some of our perceptions come from deception,
that's why we feel so strong to do the wrong thing,
thinking it's right. This is a big problem in the church
today. Ask God for wisdom over deception.

Daily Prayer

_____

_____

_____

_____

_____

DECEMBER 5TH

TRANSFORMATIONAL MEDITATIONS

Daily Prayer

_____

_____

_____

_____

_____

"Scripture for the Day"
Nehemiah Chapters 5-9

PHRASE OF THE DAY

Distract means to separate or divide by strife or disagreement.
Don't be distracted in this season, don't miss the move
of God, because you are angry with someone.

DECEMBER 6TH

TRANSFORMATIONAL MEDITATIONS

"Scripture for the Day"
Psalm Chapters 140-142

PHRASE OF THE DAY

Jesus is the gateway to heaven. If a man tries to get
in any other way, he will be considered a thief and
a robber. The front door is used to gain authorized
access in most homes. If I come looking in your back
window you might become a little concerned.

Daily Prayer

DECEMBER 7TH

TRANSFORMATIONAL MEDITATIONS

Daily Prayer

_____

_____

_____

_____

_____

"Scripture for the Day"
Song of Solomon Chapters 1-2

PHRASE OF THE DAY

Holding on to an offense of unforgiveness is like wanting
to collect on a debt against someone who owes you.
You expect payment of some sort, whether money or
misery. However, it is unrighteous for us as children of
God to avenge ourselves. Repay no one evil for evil.

DECEMBER 8TH

TRANSFORMATIONAL MEDITATIONS

"Scripture for the Day"
Revelations Chapters 1-6

PHRASE OF THE DAY

Your will is the strongest thing you have. Don't let
your will agree with them but with HIM. Then, you can
be in perfect peace in the midst of despair. Don't set
yourself up like the servant that received a full pardon
from his debt and then did not give the same to one who
owed him. This debt I am talking about is forgiveness.
Share this Word with an angry friend, Amen.
Read Matthew 18:21-35

Daily Prayer

DECEMBER 9TH

TRANSFORMATIONAL MEDITATIONS

Daily Prayer

_____

_____

_____

_____

_____

"Scripture for the Day"
Acts Chapters 21-22

_____

PHRASE OF THE DAY

Change means to make the form, nature, or
content of something different. To transform or
convert. Receiving Christ does not change you
but doing God's Word and work will, Amen.

DECEMBER 10TH

TRANSFORMATIONAL MEDITATIONS

"Scripture for the Day"
The Book of 2nd John

PHRASE OF THE DAY

Whatever you are going through at this time, remember
that God is in control and you can confidently follow
Christ. The peace of God shall overtake you.

Daily Prayer

_____

_____

_____

_____

_____

DECEMBER 11TH

TRANSFORMATIONAL MEDITATIONS

Daily Prayer

_____

_____

_____

_____

_____

"Scripture for the Day"
Deuteronomy Chapters 26-28

PHRASE OF THE DAY

You are in charge of your life; therefore no one can take it from you unless you give it away. Don't give it away to anything that exalts itself above God. Give it only to God.

DECEMBER 12TH

TRANSFORMATIONAL MEDITATIONS

"Scripture for the Day"
Nehemiah Chapters 10-13

PHRASE OF THE DAY

Redemption means an act of redeeming, deliverance, rescue,
repurchase as of something sold, recovery by payment.
We have redemption from sin through Christ, Jesus.

Daily Prayer

DECEMBER 13TH

TRANSFORMATIONAL MEDITATIONS

Daily Prayer

_____

_____

_____

_____

_____

"Scripture for the Day"
Psalm Chapters 143-145

_____

PHRASE OF THE DAY

Self-condemnation is a sin. So, when you beat yourself up
after asking God to forgive you, what is that? I speak in your
life right now, condemnation, GO IN JESUS' NAME!

DECEMBER 14TH

TRANSFORMATIONAL MEDITATIONS

"Scripture for the Day"
Song of Solomon Chapters 3-4

PHRASE OF THE DAY

Listen, quit worrying about your warfare, see
beyond it by praising God, because no weapon or
warfare formed against you shall prosper.
Let go and let God.

Daily Prayer

_____

_____

_____

_____

_____

DECEMBER 15TH

TRANSFORMATIONAL MEDITATIONS

Daily Prayer

_____

_____

_____

_____

_____

"Scripture for the Day"
Revelations Chapters 7-11

PHRASE OF THE DAY

When you are confident that God will protect you, you won't try to protect yourself. We say and do things that grieve God while defending ourselves. You are not accountable to God for what people say and do to you, but you are responsible to God for your own actions. Obedience is better than sacrifice.

DECEMBER 16TH

TRANSFORMATIONAL MEDITATIONS

"Scripture for the Day"
Acts Chapters 23-24

PHRASE OF THE DAY

You can't get into the next season with the belief
that you have now. You have to receive and believe
revelation knowledge to get to the next level. Ask God
to increase your knowledge and then walk in the new.

Daily Prayer

_____

_____

_____

_____

_____

DECEMBER 17TH

TRANSFORMATIONAL MEDITATIONS

Daily Prayer

_____

_____

_____

_____

_____

"Scripture for the Day"
The Book of 3rd John

_____

PHRASE OF THE DAY

Captivity means the state or period of being held imprisoned, enslaved or confined. Jesus came and took captivity captive and freed us. My people are now in captivity from lack of knowledge, pride, and unforgiveness. See what Jesus has done for you, move now into this new season and LEAVE the old behind.

DECEMBER 18TH

TRANSFORMATIONAL MEDITATIONS

"Scripture for the Day"
Deuteronomy Chapters 29-31

PHRASE OF THE DAY

Talking about what irritates you keeps the fire of anger going.
Refusing to discuss it cuts the fuel and makes the fire die out.
Talk more about the solution.

Daily Prayer

DECEMBER 19TH

TRANSFORMATIONAL MEDITATIONS

Daily Prayer

_____

_____

_____

_____

_____

"Scripture for the Day"
Esther Chapters 1-5

PHRASE OF THE DAY

The only way you will get out of your valley is to look
and walk towards the hills, from which comes your
help. Be diligent to please the Lord, not man.

DECEMBER 20TH

TRANSFORMATIONAL MEDITATIONS

"Scripture for the Day"
Psalm Chapters 146-148

PHRASE OF THE DAY

We all have been issued a measure of faith, just as we all
have been issued a measure of muscle. What has been issued
is up to the person to develop. Your development is your
responsibility, it is highly recommended to seek good counsel.
Faith and muscle have the ability to grow if you work at it.

Daily Prayer

_____

_____

_____

_____

_____

DECEMBER 21ST

TRANSFORMATIONAL MEDITATIONS

Daily Prayer

_____

_____

_____

_____

_____

"Scripture for the Day"
Song of Solomon Chapters 5-6

_____

PHRASE OF THE DAY

Pharisees are religious leaders and Torah scholars in charge
of holding other people and not themselves, to the law.
Accuser of the brethren and lovers of money, will not receive
correction. The Spirit of the Lord will be dealing with
religious leaders this year. Repent and have compassion.

DECEMBER 22 [ND]

TRANSFORMATIONAL MEDITATIONS

"Scripture for the Day"
Revelations Chapters 12-17

PHRASE OF THE DAY

A stronghold is a thought process impregnated by a
spiritual force that keeps you in bondage. These thoughts
raise themselves up above and against the knowledge
of Christ. Strongholds are formed during times of
distress, trauma, or need. Satan may offer you a way
that leaves out God, but bondage will surely follow.

Daily Prayer

_____

_____

_____

_____

_____

DECEMBER 23RD

TRANSFORMATIONAL MEDITATIONS

Daily Prayer

_____

_____

_____

_____

_____

"Scripture for the Day"
Acts Chapters 25-26

PHRASE OF THE DAY

Being loved is the most powerful motivation in the
world. Our ability to love is shaped by our experience of
love. We usually love others as we have been loved.

DECEMBER 24TH

TRANSFORMATIONAL MEDITATIONS

"Scripture for the Day"
The Book of Jude

PHRASE OF THE DAY

When His blood is the doorpost of our lives, God
delivers us from the destroyer. We are redeemed by
the Blood of the Lamb and from our enemies, so,
let's represent God correctly by acting like it.

Daily Prayer

DECEMBER 25TH

TRANSFORMATIONAL MEDITATIONS

Daily Prayer

_____

_____

_____

_____

_____

"Scripture for the Day"
Deuteronomy Chapters 32-34

PHRASE OF THE DAY

She will bear a son and you shall call his name Jesus, for
He will save His people from their sins. Matthew 1:21

DECEMBER 26TH

TRANSFORMATIONAL MEDITATIONS

"Scripture for the Day"
Esther Chapters 6-10

PHRASE OF THE DAY

False teachers love to cause strife and division by arguing over Godless chatter. This coming year, be sure to stay away from those that quarrel about words that add no value to you.

Daily Prayer

_____

_____

_____

_____

_____

DECEMBER 27TH

TRANSFORMATIONAL MEDITATIONS

Daily Prayer

_____

_____

_____

_____

_____

"Scripture for the Day"
Psalm Chapters 149-150

PHRASE OF THE DAY

The glory of God cannot flow through a vessel lacking
self-control. Find strength in God's Word.

DECEMBER 28TH

TRANSFORMATIONAL MEDITATIONS

"Scripture for the Day"
Song of Solomon Chapters 7-8

PHRASE OF THE DAY

When we intentionally develop our character with trials, we strengthen our frailties, tame our vices, and prepare ourselves to fulfill our personal leadership. You have to move forward no matter what mood you feel you're in.

Daily Prayer

_____

_____

_____

_____

_____

DECEMBER 29TH

TRANSFORMATIONAL MEDITATIONS

Daily Prayer

_____

_____

_____

_____

_____

"Scripture for the Day"
Revelations Chapters 18-22

PHRASE OF THE DAY

Every decision we act on adds a sentence, paragraph, or chapter to our life story, which someone will read one day. The ultimate audience is God, Jesus, and the Holy Spirit, who determine where we will spend eternity. We are in control of our story and it will not be a mistake when we spend eternity in Heaven. It will be very intentional. Our values, ethics, and moral principles protect our hope of glory from being destroyed or sidelined.

DECEMBER 30TH

TRANSFORMATIONAL MEDITATIONS

"Scripture for the Day"
Acts Chapters 27

PHRASE OF THE DAY

Your past was designed to build you, not kill you.
Reading this message is proof that you're not dead. I
command that every leech that has been attached to you
will catch fire and burn now. I apply fresh anointed oil
to those wounds. Receive it in Jesus' name, Amen.

Daily Prayer

DECEMBER 31ST

TRANSFORMATIONAL MEDITATIONS

Daily Prayer

_____

_____

_____

_____

_____

"Scripture for the Day"
Acts Chapters 28

PHRASE OF THE DAY

When you change (are transformed) everything that wants
to relate with you either has to change or move on.

As for me and my house we will serve the Lord. Joshua 24:15